CAREER DEVELOPMENT AND PLANNING

Further titles in the McGraw-Hill Training Series

THE BUSINESS OF TRAINING
Achieving Success in Changing World Markets
Trevor Bentley ISBN 0-07-707328-2

EVALUATING TRAINING EFFECTIVENESS
Translating Theory into Practice
Peter Bramley ISBN 0-07-707331-2

DEVELOPING EFFECTIVE TRAINING SKILLS
Tony Pont ISBN 0-07-707383-5

MAKING MANAGEMENT DEVELOPMENT WORK
Achieving Success in the Nineties
Charles Margerison ISBN 0-07-707382-7

MANAGING PERSONAL LEARNING AND CHANGE
A Trainer's Guide
Neil Clark ISBN 0-07-707344-4

HOW TO DESIGN EFFECTIVE TEXT-BASED OPEN LEARNING:
A Modular Course
Nigel Harrison ISBN 0-07-707355-X

HOW TO DESIGN EFFECTIVE COMPUTER BASED TRAINING:
A Modular Course
Nigel Harrison ISBN 0-07-707354-1

HOW TO SUCCEED IN EMPLOYEE DEVELOPMENT
Moving from Vision to Results
Ed Moorby ISBN 0-07-707459-9

DEVELOPING WOMEN THROUGH TRAINING
A Practical Handbook
Liz Willis and
Jenny Daisley ISBN 0-07-707566-8

USING VIDEO IN TRAINING AND EDUCATION
Ashly Pinnington ISBN 0-07-707384-3

TRANSACTIONAL ANALYSIS FOR TRAINERS
Julie Hay ISBN 0-07-707470-X

SALES TRAINING
A Guide to Developing Effective Sales People
Frank S. Salisbury ISBN 0-07-707458-0

SELF-DEVELOPMENT
A Facilitator's Guide
David Megginson and
Mike Pedler ISBN 0-07-707460-2

TOTAL QUALITY TRAINING
The Quality Culture and Quality Trainer
Brian Thomas ISBN 0-07-707472-6

Details of these and other titles in the series are available from:

The Product Manager, Professional Books, McGraw-Hill Book Company Europe,
Shoppenhangers Road, Maidenhead, Berkshire, SL6 2QL.
Telephone: 0628 23432 Fax: 0628 770224

Career development and planning

A guide for managers, trainers and personnel staff

Malcolm Peel

McGRAW-HILL BOOK COMPANY

London · New York · St Louis · San Francisco · Auckland
Bogotá · Caracas · Hamburg · Lisbon · Madrid · Mexico · Milan
Montreal · New Delhi · Panama · Paris · San Juan · São Paulo
Singapore · Sydney · Tokyo · Toronto

Published by
McGRAW-HILL Book Company Europe
Shoppenhangers Road, Maidenhead, Berkshire, SL6 2QL, England.
Telephone: 0628 23432
Fax: 0628 770224

British Library Cataloguing in Publication Data
Peel, Malcolm
  Career development and planning.
  I. Title
  331.702

  ISBN 0-07-707554-4

Library of Congress Cataloging-in-Publication Data
Peel, Malcolm.
  Career development and planning: a guide for managers, trainers,
and personnel staff / Malcolm Peel.
    p.   cm. — (McGraw-Hill training series)
  Includes bibliographical references.
  ISBN 0-07-707554-4 (P/B)
  1. Career development. 2. Personnel management. I. Title.
II. Series.
HF5549.C35P44   1992
658.3'124—dc20   91-42433

12345 CL 95432

Typeset by Book Ens Limited, Baldock, Herts
Printed and bound in Great Britain by Clays Ltd, St Ives plc

Contents

Series preface

Training and development are now firmly centre stage in most organizations, if not all. Nothing unusual in that—for some organizations. They have always seen training and development as part of the heart of their businesses—but more and more must see it the same way.

The demographic trends through the nineties will inject into the marketplace severe competition for good people who will need good training. Young people without conventional qualifications, skilled workers in redundant crafts, people out of work, women wishing to return to work—all will require excellent training to fit them to meet the job demands of the 1990s and beyond.

But excellent training does not spring from what we have done well in the past. T&D specialists are in a new ball game. 'Maintenance' training—training to keep up skill levels to do what we have always done—will be less in demand. Rather, organization, work and market change training are now much more important and will remain so for some time. Changing organizations and people is no easy task, requiring special skills and expertise which, sadly, many T&D specialists do not possess.

To work as a 'change' specialist requires us to get to centre stage—to the heart of the company's business. This means we have to ask about future goals and strategies and even be involved in their development, at least as far as T&D policies are concerned.

This demands excellent communication skills, political expertise, negotiating ability, diagnostic skills—indeed, all the skills a good internal consultant requires.

The implications for T&D specialists are considerable. It is not enough merely to be skilled in the basics of training, we must also begin to act like business people and to think in business terms and talk the language of business. We must be able to resource training not just from within but by using the vast array of external resources. We must be able to manage our activities as well as any other manager. We must share in the creation and communication of the company's vision. We must never let the goals of the company out of our sight.

In short, we may have to grow and change with the business. It will be hard. We shall not only have to demonstrate relevance but also value for money and achievement of results. We shall be our own boss, as accountable for results as any other line manager, and we shall have to deal with fewer internal resources.

The challenge is on, as many T&D specialists have demonstrated to me over the past few years. We need to be capable of meeting that challenge. This is why McGraw-Hill Book Company Europe have planned and launched this major new training series—to help us meet that challenge.

The series covers all aspects of T&D and provides the knowledge base from which we can develop plans to meet the challenge. They are practical books for the professional person. They are a starting point for planning our journey into the twenty-first century.

Use them well. Don't just read them. Highlight key ideas, thoughts, action pointers or whatever, and have a go at doing something with them. Through experimentation we evolve; through stagnation we die.

I know that all the authors in the McGraw-Hill Training Series would want me to wish you good luck. Have a great journey into the twenty-first century.

ROGER BENNETT
Series Editor

About the series editor

Roger Bennett has over 20 years' experience in training, management education, research and consulting. He has long been involved with trainer training and trainer effectiveness. He has carried out research into trainer effectiveness and conducted workshops, seminars and conferences on the subject around the world. He has written extensively on the subject including the book *Improving Trainer Effectiveness*, Gower. His work has taken him all over the world and has involved directors of companies as well as managers and trainers.

Dr Bennett has worked in engineering, several business schools (including the International Management Centre, where he launched the UK's first masters degree in T&D) and has been a board director of two companies. He is the editor of the *Journal of European Industrial Training* and was series editor of the ITD's *Get In There* workbook and video package for the managers of training departments. He now runs his own business called The Management Development Consultancy.

Acknowledgements

I find it difficult to acknowledge all the help I have received in writing this book as it has come from so many sources and in so many ways. I have gained it from all the sources named in the References with each chapter and in the Bibliography. Chapter 2 benefited particularly from Bill Roger's handbook *Careers Education and Guidance* (CRAC, 1984).

The patient and knowledgeable staff of the Management Information Centre of the British Institute of Management have, as on so many previous occasions, been especially helpful and given unsparingly of their time and expertise. John Robins of BIM made many particularly helpful comments and suggestions. Jeff Pell of the Northamptonshire Careers Service was invaluable in clarifying my understanding of the role of the Service. Alison Straw of BIM, apart from tolerating endless mutterings about whatever difficulty happened to be uppermost on my mind, helped my understanding of the role of counselling in career development and helped me with several sources. Sue Wood, of the Institute of Personnel Management, drew my attention to the importance of the concept of continuous development and kindly gave permission to use several sources. Elsa Davies of BIM read Chapter 2, Initial career choice, and made helpful suggestions and comments on it. My son Richard has continued to act as an unpaid word-processing consultant.

To all these—and to any I may have, unwittingly, I promise—forgotten, I offer my most sincere thanks.

MALCOLM PEEL

Introduction

Sound career development is a must today for individual, organization and nation.

How are careers really developed?

There are those, of course, who regard career development as a simple, single-minded activity. A quick run-round a few colleagues produced the following sure-fire recommendations:

- careful choice of parents
- marrying the boss' daughter (or son, as the case may be)
- wearing the right old school or club tie
- nepotism
- brazen exploitation of friends in high places
- ensuring you are in the right place at the right time
- joining a powerful secret society
- laughing at the boss' jokes
- being always ready to stab a friend in the back.

The aim of this book

This book does not pretend to develop such valuable but specialized skills as these; rather it seeks to survey the broader, if less exciting, ground of *real* career development. It looks at the influences and techniques that have a bearing on every stage of the career—from schooldays to retirement. There are many of these—perhaps more than we generally realize. There are also many players in the game; the individual concerned, that person's parents and friends, teacher, manager, the human resources professionals at that person's place of work, politicians, bureaucrats and society as a whole.

This book has been written from the angle of the human resources professional, but I believe that most of what is suggested will also interest managers and anybody working at progressing their own career.

Each chapter (except 12 and 13) concludes with an Action check-list. Most items in these lists are expressed from the angle of the trainer, but many are equally appropriate for other managers.

While I have done all I can to check that the facts given in this book are the latest ones, career development is a highly political and particularly fluid area and so there can be no guarantee that they are current or up to date in all particulars.

1 What is career development?

'Career', 'development' and 'career development' need to be defined and their implications need to be explored. Career development is of great importance to individuals, organizations and society as a whole. Although other forms of development exist within organizations, all overlap with but are distinct from career development.

What is a 'career'?

By derivation, a career is the path something or someone has taken; in a race, a horse 'careers along'. In the occupational context, it may mean our chosen occupation, craft or profession: 'He is a career politician'; 'My chosen career is law'.

However, it may also include occupations as well as paid jobs. As a mother, Nichola Evans writes to the *Independent*:[1]

. . . I do resent the constant adverse publicity that my chosen career receives and the implication that all women are dying to get back to 'real' work. Bringing up two small children is the most rewarding and stimulating job I have ever done.

With so many possible uses of 'career', the most useful definition seems to be the broadest. *The Shorter Oxford Dictionary* defines 'career' simply as:

A person's course or progress through life

thus including paid and voluntary employment (whether full or part-time), self-employment, domestic roles and periods out of paid employment.

How much does the career matter?

There is a danger that a 'career' may be seen as a middle-class concept and, indeed, it is sometimes suggested that neither the unskilled nor the high-born have any use for this idea. There is enough truth in this for one to ask, legitimately, 'Does everyone actually *want* a career?'

Careers are important to their owners for many reasons: to earn enough to keep themselves and their families, to appear respectable, to give status, because everyone else has one or to achieve personal fulfilment. The motivation can be positive—ambition, the desire to excel, to push forward frontiers or to benefit the human race—or negative—jealousy of close relatives or of the world in general, dissatisfaction, even hate.

The value individuals place on their own career varies widely. For some it is the most important aspect of their life, for which they are prepared to sacrifice personal, family and leisure interests, even health. At the other extreme drop-outs of all sorts reject not only a structured career but the very concept of work within an economic framework. Most of us fall between these extremes, placing our career and its development among, but not necessarily at the top of, our life objectives.

The importance of the career and its development is often assumed to correlate with potential—the greater someone's ability, the greater that person's concern with their career. While this may sometimes be true, it must not be taken to imply that those of less proven ability are not capable of being deeply concerned about their careers.

One of the most dangerous fallacies is the belief that women are less concerned about their careers than men. In fact, women must often struggle far harder to realize comparable career goals than men, although too many find the combined problems of motherhood and social attitudes insuperable. Many women regard motherhood as a valid and integral part of their career, as evidenced by Nichola Evans' letter earlier.

Age can affect the importance people attach to their careers. Typically, it has greater importance for younger people and this diminishes from some point in middle life, but generalization here is dangerous and unhelpful.

Lack of encouragement and opportunity for career development within employment may lead to people channelling their energy and skills into leisure, political and community activities. Some office-holders in clubs and societies, local councillors, community and social activists and magistrates may include those who have experienced unsatisfying career development in employment.

Whose career is it anyway?

The principal owner of a career is the person experiencing it. However, because most careers involve employment, employers have a vested interest in the careers of their employees and a degree of shared ownership in their development. This partnership (for that is what it must be) can either be a source of mutual support or destructive tension.

The nature of the career partnership will vary depending on the size of the organization. Large organizations tend to base career development on the assumption that employees will stay with them. Within smaller organizations, career development often presents problems because of lack of internal opportunities, resources and, occasionally, understanding of its importance. This may mean that changes of employer are essential for successful development.

Nobody is an island. For the unemployed, self-employed or unpaid worker, such as full-time housewife or mother, the career partnership is subsumed in other partnerships—with spouse, children or friends. In this situation, career development is in the owner's hands to a greater extent than if that person were employed. However, the profound effects career decisions have on others will always give them a right to be involved.

Career changes

Within the UK there was for a long time a tendency to regard life-long employment with a single employer as the career norm. However, this picture becomes less and less the norm year by year. By the start of the nineties, typical careers involve between three and five employers—sometimes many more and an increasing number of individuals are experiencing periods of self- or unemployment.

The general culture of a society also has its effect. Career development in Japan, for example, where employees rarely change employer, is fundamentally different from career development in the USA, where a 'hire and fire' culture is endemic.

For an increasing number, there may even be one or more changes of career direction and technical obsolescence is an unavoidable threat for those who do not change.

Career structure

Structured organizations provide and expect structured careers. The armed forces recruit at set ages, move personnel through a rigid structure of ranks, training for each move, and retire them at set ages, depending upon rank. The career patterns of the self-employed, on the other hand, vary widely. Most commercial organizations lie somewhere between these boundaries, with careers in the larger and more structured companies bearing a closer resemblance to the military model and careers in smaller organizations having more in common with those of the self-employed.

In thinking about career development, we must not assume that the structured, military model is the target; well-developed careers come in an infinite variety of forms.

The phases of the career

Careers are often thought of as a succession of phases and many suggestions have been put forward along these lines by writers on career development. Charles Healey[2] speaks of five stages of life:

1 growth (0–14 years of age)
2 exploration (15–24 years of age)
3 establishment (25–44 years of age)
4 maintenance (45–65 years of age)
5 decline (65+ years of age).

James W. Walker[3] lists four similar phases:

1 establishing identity
2 growing and getting established
3 maintenance of and adjustment to self
4 decline.

There may be more dangers than advantages in such models, however. While career patterns within large organizations are more likely to follow a stratified, military model, those within smaller organizations, the self-employed and those caring for families are not. The increasing frequency of major changes in career direction also break any rigid mould. Any suggestion of inflexible age bands is particularly unrealistic and dangerous.

Development

The word 'develop' is frequently used transitively. We can develop our muscles, develop a film, develop an argument or a new system. It is hard, dedicated work, with a clear target in view that we will know when we have reached it.

'Develop' also means 'to foster' and 'to cultivate'. These are less precise activities, capable of being approached in an infinite number of ways and leading to infinite (if not sometimes unmeasurable) degrees of success. Such activities have a strong overtone of do-gooding about them. The skilled gardener will help the plants to grow, but will do little to dictate their shape and nothing to alter their inborn characteristics. The gardener's skill lies in knowing as much as possible about what these are likely to be and giving them whatever help is required.

The word is also frequently used intransitively; 'he developed rapidly in that job'. As managers or human resources professionals we may aim to improve the chances for an individual's development, but that person alone can do the developing—we can only facilitate the process by creating the right climate and offering incentives to encourage individuals to develop themselves.

Human resources professionals and managers must, like the gardener, understand the soil, climate and aspect of his garden, landscape it, select suitable plants, prepare the ground for them and plant them carefully and at the right time. Then they must be fed, watered, talked to and thinned out, ensuring all have sufficient space to grow. They will also need to be weeded and everything must be done to prevent or cure diseases. All this without forcing plants too far or too fast or trying to make them grow in a particular way, or indeed at all.

Career development

Putting 'career' and 'development' together, we can say that career development is the life-long process of fostering and cultivating the shape of the individual's working life so as to make best use of inherent talents, skills, knowledge and interests for that person's and (if there is one) the employer's benefit and also to match it as closely as possible to the other aspects of the person's life.

As such, it is a forward-looking activity, aiming at the medium and long term. It is concerned with potential—the potential of individuals and of the situations in which they are or may be. It looks backwards only in the sense that everyone must start from where they are and try to learn from their mistakes. History is not exactly bunk in career development, but it is of fairly limited value.

The term career development often carries a strong overtone of promotion and upward movement as to 'develop a career' is often taken to mean reaching a higher salary level, but for most people, most of the time, *real* upward movement is neither practicable nor desirable. Either the opportunity is not there or they are not fit, or do not wish, to take it. Career development makes an individual's *present* job situation more satisfying and makes that person more effective to the employer (if there is one)—it does not necessarily imply promotion.

The resources available to the individual and the organization in this process include:

- the education system at every level
- the organizational human resource specialists
- government and private advisory agencies
- literature and open learning aids
- the individual's professional institution (if there is one)
- the individual's manager, peer group, family and friends

and, above all, the individual's own abilities and personality.

Some see development as occurring at random points in time as a result of 'critical incidents'. Most of us, contemplating our own career, will probably identify certain events or periods of critical importance, for better or worse, in its growth or lack thereof; meeting or working for a specific individual, for example, participating in a particular training event or simply being in the right place at the right time.

The importance of career development

The development of careers is vital to the individual, the organization and to society as a whole. It is also the core of human resources work: to see the results of career development in the individual is to obtain one of the deepest satisfactions a manager or a human resources professional can experience.

Benefits for the individual

Maslow's well-known 'hierarchy of needs' places self-actualization firmly at the top of the pyramid as the goal to which all will, given satisfaction of their more basic needs, aspire. The development and planning of the career is central to this self-actualization. It will contribute at the deepest level to working effectiveness, motivation, and personal fulfilment, not only improving working life but spreading into the social, leisure, family and personal spheres. Lack of such satisfactions is one of the most potent causes of stress.

Benefits for the employer

The benefits are of equal importance to the employer. If the purpose of an organization is to produce profits, then the best-developed people will help it to produce the greatest profit. Employees only give of their best when placed in the right job, given the right development and training, supported by the best management and with the most suitable opportunities for growth. Unduly stressed and unhappy employees will be less efficient than those who find the match between job, career and personality satisfying. An organization that exploits staff and denies them development opportunities may prosper in the short term but will, sooner or later, be overtaken by those that make the fullest use of their human resources.

Employees who have full support in the development of their career will work better in their present job. The organization is also more likely to retain them. Their potential will then be available for other roles within the organization and their growing skills, knowledge and commitment may become crucial to the organization's own growth and development.

The accelerating rate of technological change makes continuous development of all employees essential. Those who fail to realize this face the alternatives of bidding for the skills they need in an ever more expensive market or seeing their operation becoming progressively outdated.

Professional competence In the professional context there is now held to be a legal duty to be up-to-date in one's knowledge. While case law has not been extended to cover those outside structured professions (except in specific areas, such as health and safety at work), many would consider continuous updating a moral obligation for all, especially managers. For this reason, most professions and their respective institutions see continuing development of their members as vital.

The social importance The economic future of the country can be seen in terms of the efficiency with which it uses its human resources. The reduction in the number of young people entering the labour market during the 1990s makes it more essential than ever that the potential of all is used. The economy will depend increasingly on the contribution of older workers— for example, women returning after child-rearing and those, at whatever stage of their working life, whose potential has not been fully realized.

Denial of opportunities for education, training and development also leads to the risk of the creation of an underclass. Social stratification has been seen as related mainly to wealth and correctable, if at all, by its redistribution. Many are now convinced that distribution of the opportunities for life-long personal development are more important and offer the best hope of avoiding an ever-widening gap between the richest and poorest in society. The social infrastructure will be put at risk as those without adequate skills become progressively less able to keep up with those who have them.

Effort given to career development is thus not a soft option—being nice to people—but essential for survival and growth to organizations and the nation itself. The choice is not whether we develop ourselves and others (development happens, for better or worse, as long as life lasts), the only choices are whether we develop positively or negatively, by accident or according to plan, comprehensively or in a limited area.

Other kinds of development

Apart from career development, the word 'development' is used in several other contexts within management. We can speak of:

- organizational development
- team development
- management development
- individual development.

Organizational development

Organizational development is a less frequently used term that has only an oblique relevance to career development. It refers to a process aimed at improving the overall effectiveness of an organization and its members by a systematic programme of change. The programme will be led by top management and often guided by consultants who intervene in appropriate ways in the processes of the organization.

Organizational development may be said to concern the same area as career development but be the opposite side of the same coin. In so far as individual careers are more likely to be satisfying and effective in an effective organization, the outcomes of organizational development will help the career development of all individuals in it.

Team development

Team development is a key activity for every manager. It is, in a sense, organizational development within the manager's own area. Although in practice it is concerned mainly with the factors of group dynamics and the interpersonal relationships within the team, it must interrelate closely with individual development (see Chapter 5 for further discussion of this topic).

Management development

This is the combination of the individual development and career development of those who are, or who are expected to become, managers.

It is tragic that the words 'management' and 'development' have become so firmly cemented together as 90 per cent of employees at any one time are not managers and most will never become managers. While the development of its managers is clearly of great importance to an organization, the development of *all* its employees, whatever their job or status, must be vital. Some organizations accept the development philosophy for their 'high-fliers' (those they see as worthy of the 'fast track') only. Some extend it to those in the middle range of their managerial and professional structure, but few apply it to *all* who work for them.

Individual development

The distinction between *individual* development and *career* development can become blurred. Indeed, the two must overlap as career development cannot take place without individual development. In developing a career, all the techniques of individual development are needed. For this reason, a good deal of the material in this book relates to both activities.

Career planning

This phrase is often used to imply action by the individual owner of the career, while 'career management' is used to describe career development activities undertaken by the organization.

A few individuals are sensible or lucky enough to produce workable long-range career plans, although such plans are always liable to be altered (for better or worse) by events. For many people, career planning is principally a matter of ambition: 'I intend to be a millionaire by the age of 30', 'I want to get into Parliament', 'I want to become a judge', and so on. While such ambitions are characteristic of younger people, some remain ambitious throughout life.

As with most other activities, the development of a career will always be enhanced by conscious planning. Although ultimately the responsibility of the individual, career planning can benefit from outside help—by the employing organization, career counsellors or a professional institution. The ways this help can be given are discussed in the appropriate chapters.

Career management

The most highly managed form of career development is probably that which exists within the commissioned ranks of the armed forces, where personnel of a specific rank will undergo training for the rank above but will only be promoted to that rank on satisfactory completion and if an appropriate vacancy arises before an age bar is reached.

Other management of individual careers is probably only systematically attempted by a few large organizations for their managers or potential managers. Where it does take place, it is normally based on a review of all those reaching a certain level, either by attendance at a standard training course or an assessment centre. The review identifies high-fliers for subsequent nurturing, often according to an individual plan. While an important aspect of career development for those so picked out, this process does nothing for the vast majority of employees and can have an adverse effect on the careers of many.

Appraisal schemes have a place in career management and planning as many are designed to identify potential. However, the track record of such schemes in this area is often not good (they are discussed more fully in Chapter 10).

To believe that careers can be planned and managed mechanistically has its dangers for the individual and the organization. Career plans are at the mercy of factors outside the control of the planner, such as emerging technological needs, commercial expansion and contraction, amalgamations, take-overs, privatizations, changes in top personnel, head-hunting by rivals, health and death itself, but these problems in no way detract from the prime importance of continuous, responsive career development.

Action check-list

- Encourage all—irrespective of status, age or sex—to work at developing their career.
- Help everyone to accept full responsibility for their own career development.
- Avoid using only a 'military' model of careers and career success.
- Take a responsive and organic rather than mechanistic view of helping individuals to develop their careers.
- Avoid thinking of 'career development' and 'promotion' as synonymous.
- Help managers at all levels to understand the benefits of the career development of their people to the organization as a whole.
- Ensure that managers and professionals understand their responsibility to remain professionally fully up to date.
- Ensure that other developmental activities contribute to career development.

References

1. Evans, Nichola, in a letter to the *Independent*, 19 January, 1991.
2. Healy, Charles C., *Career Development* (Allyn and Bacon Inc., Boston, 1982).
3. Walker, James W., *Human Resource Planning* (McGraw-Hill, 1980).

2 Initial career choice

Initial career choice is often not rational and will always be subject to many long- and short-term pressures. These include the effects of family and upbringing, every stage of education, experience of the world of work and formal sources of career advice.

The professional trainer is able to influence this process at a number of points and is often at the forefront of efforts to inform and attract recruits into the organization and industry.

Rational career choices?

Someone I know made her initial career choice by leaving school one morning rather than admit she had not done her history homework. Even though the initial choice of career is one of the two or three most important decisions an individual ever makes, it is rarely made rationally and often results from purely random pressures at the critical point in time. Apart from incompleted homework, it may flow from a shortage of cash; a quarrel with parents, teacher or partner; a chance meeting or remark; a TV programme or eye-catching advertisement.

Theoretically, the individual should define their objectives, bearing in mind their skills, interests, ambitions, achievements, limitations, qualifications and desired life-style. They should then generate a list of possible careers, obtain information about each and establish which one best meets their objectives. Such a process, however, while it is conceptually sound, is usually influenced by the complexities and pressures of real life.

Career choice influences

The factors influencing career choice include:

- family
- society
- educational experience
- experience of the world of work
- formal sources of career advice
- the employer's role.

We may feel that there is little we can do to affect the way these factors operate, but the more we understand their working, the better our perspective on later career stages. In fact, we can have an input for each.

As parents we will be involved with our own children; as private individuals, we can contribute to the national debate and general climate of opinion; as professionals, we will have opportunities for direct involvement.

Family The process of initial career choice begins at birth, if not before. The financial position, social status, attitudes, beliefs and occupational history of parents and family are the inescapable starting points for career development.

To be born with a silver spoon in one's mouth is usually an advantage when the time comes to choose a career. Parental income and the way it is used (say, private education and the general life-style of the family) will be major influences.

The children of working-class families remain less likely to stay in education after the compulsory minimum leaving age than those of higher income groups, despite the financial support available, thus impoverishing their field of career choice. This is one component in the 'cycle of deprivation' that blights the career options of some young people from generation to generation—equality of opportunity within the UK is still only a partly realized dream. The attempts of politicians, working through the mechanisms of taxation, the support of the welfare state and changes to the educational system have achieved less than most would have hoped. While social mobility (measured as the extent of change between the occupational classification of parents and children) has increased in the UK over the last century, the pace of change has slackened since the Second World War.

Fewer companies are now named '. . . and Son', although the tradition of the family business will never die. However, family tradition is not restricted to business ownership. In some families employment has continued in the same industry—even with the same employer—for generations. Railway families, for example, have provided engine drivers or signalmen from generation to generation. In recent years many such chains have been broken; 'Whatever you do, don't follow in my footsteps', parents have advised their children. For their part, children have increasingly felt the need to gain their freedom by rejecting the life-style, preferences and advice of their parents.

The effects of the 'old boy' network are probably less strong in most areas now than in the past. Where they do exist, they will take the time-honoured form of a word in the ear of a senior colleague or associate, contact with a personal friend (whether from school, college or some other context) or perhaps the obtaining of a necessary union card.

Society Social pressures outside the circle of the family operate through peer groups, perceived social class, national politics and the media.

The options considered and the preconceptions held by individual members will be affected by the norms of any group to which they belong. Peer groups inevitably have an influence both in initial career choice and later development.

Perceptions of class limit career choices. Few who think of themselves as working class would consider the possibility of becoming, for example, a barrister or a stockbroker; few who see themselves as upper middle class look seriously at such careers as lorry driver or retail tobacconist.

Political influence may be significant. Opinions about the way the national economy should operate and the importance of, for example, manufacturing industry, enterprise, profit and the caring professions, generate a climate of opinion that will affect individuals' initial career choice.

Media influence can occasionally be great. The BBC TV series 'All creatures great and small' is said to have influenced the career choice of many young people, as witnessed by the numbers applying for veterinary training at the peak of its popularity. The effect of programmes depicting, for example, police or customs work may also be measurable and a popular actor or actress playing a strongly occupationally-oriented role can set youngsters applying for the same career by the thousand.

Using the media to provide a correct picture of the career opportunities in our own industry or profession may be easier than we realize. Local radio stations are always delighted to establish links with local industry and local papers are avid for well-informed articles about the local world of work. Even the national media are open to authoritative and well-produced contributions on items of current interest.

Educational experience 'It is the role of education to push people on.' Few doubt the importance of education in a society in which needs, values and technology are continuously shifting, but there has been much heart searching about the relationship between education and careers—in the UK, particularly since the so-called 'Great Debate' on the subject initiated by the then Prime Minister, James Callaghan, in 1977. While a number of initiatives took place (for example, the setting up of the Manpower Services Commission, then the Training Agency and now Training and Enterprise Councils), they have met with only qualified success.

Although some feel the world of education is claustrophobic, closed and inbred, there are many opportunities to influence it. The more interest parents display in the education of their children—both in the home and by building relationships with school and teachers—the more successful that education is likely to be. The scope for direct influence through membership of boards and governors and parent-teacher associations has been greatly increased since the Education Act 1981. Equally, most schools welcome contacts with local employers and managers, and many companies, such as Marks and Spencer and Lloyds, respond by giving talks, allowing children to 'work shadow' managers and so on.

In the UK, there has been continued pressure in recent years to make school education more vocational in character and to provide the know-

ledge and skills needed by individuals to earn their living and contribute
to the economy. It has been generally held that many young people
leave the education system without the basic skills of numeracy and literacy. This has resulted, among other changes, in the development of
the National Curriculum, designed to ensure a basic grounding in all
subjects, such as English and mathematics, agreed to be essential for
occupational effectiveness, the Youth Training Scheme and Employment
Training.

Both educationalists and industrialists accept that there is a delicate balance to be struck between liberal studies and those that are directly
vocational and that if educational content and the need to create wealth
drift too far apart, no one will, in the long term, benefit.

Every stage of the education process affects career choice.

Infant/primary education 'Give me a child until the age of eight, and I will have him for life', said
the Jesuits, and most people agree. Career choice may be deeply
affected by educational experience at primary, infant or even nursery
level.

It is during this phase of education that socialization occurs, and role
stereotypes are established. The way in which competitiveness, cooperation, attitudes to authority, discipline, group norms and leadership
styles are approached will have lasting influences on career choice and
subsequent success. In particular, the roles of male and female are
largely set during this phase. If in the nursery the doctors are all male
and the nurses all female, or the boy always goes out to work and the
dutiful girl always stays at home in the wendy house, these children's
games may colour attitudes and behaviour life-long.

Teachers' attitudes to the sexes are vital. In a recent study by Dr Jane
French[1] evidence is presented of sexist bias in favour of boys by both
male and female teachers. Dr French found that boys, on average,
received two thirds of the teacher's attention and girls only a third. She
expresses particular concern about the effect of such bias on girls with
working-class backgrounds in the lower streams.

The effectiveness of teaching methods cannot be ignored. The
technicalities of teaching reading, for example, or basic arithmetic, seem
likely to remain a subject of doubt and controversy both within and outside the teaching profession, but there is no disagreement that a failure
to develop the level of skill needed for career success must be a disaster.

Middle/secondary education The secondary school environment influences career choice through its
overall culture, the attitudes of individual teachers, the mechanism for
subject choice, and the direct work of career teachers. In many schools,
industry has been regarded as a career for those who have failed.

Although the schools inspectorate, in their response to Government
proposals on the school curriculum, said that systematic career educa-

tion should begin no later than the third secondary year, it is rare for this to happen. However, the implications of subject choices at this stage (for example, choosing between arts or science subjects) may be fundamental to subsequent career choice. Often the information necessary for a rational decision is not available and it will be based on factors such as course availability, the pupil's skill, interest and previous success, the teacher's reputation and the relationship between pupil and teacher.

Course availability must depend on the teaching and physical resources of the school and may prove a limiting factor, especially at sixth-form level and for subjects requiring expensive equipment. This is an area in which local employers can make a direct contribution through the donation of equipment and supporting expertise. The opportunity to generate interest in their line of business can help to stimulate career choices that will help their recruitment needs.

Most secondary schools appoint one or more teachers to give career advice. A smaller number spread responsibility for vocational guidance more widely among senior staff. Many allocate a classroom or other area for the permanent display of career literature and other material. Talks in school may be arranged from employers or organizations such as the local Chamber of Commerce, a Junior Chamber, a Rotary Club, Round Table or the Soroptimists. When time and opportunity allow, visits may be arranged to local employers' premises and work shadowing of managers might take place. The CBI's 'Understanding British Industry' (UBI), a series of one-day presentations by industrialists and managers to conferences of older school pupils organized on a local basis across the country, also continues to have an impact.

It is unfortunate that, despite individual dedication and enthusiasm, many careers teachers and school career activities do less than they would like to help the initial career choice of their pupils. The resources available are often extremely limited, both in the space available for career rooms and the gathering and storage of material, and the curriculum time available. Even so, some schools do manage to arrange work experience periods for older pupils.

Careers teachers almost always continue classroom teaching and thus have insufficient time to gather material, contacts and experience and to share these with their pupils. A recent survey by MORI of 18- to 34-year-olds, for example, found that 92 per cent would have preferred more careers guidance. Typically, one lady recalled that she had had,

. . . just one 10-minute period of careers advice during my whole time at school, when I was asked: 'Do you want to be a nurse or a teacher?'[2]

Lack of resources also results in career advice being concentrated on the last years of school, when critical and limiting subject choices have already been made.

Liaison between the Careers Service and school teachers can also be a difficult area. Subconsciously, some teachers may still see the Careers Service under its old name of the Juvenile Employment Service, and its careers officers as Placement Officers whose aim is to guide pupils into employment and away from the sixth form.

Most sadly of all, very few teachers have experience outside the educational system on which they can base their advice. Schemes now exist that provide short periods of secondment for practising teachers, but the value of these is inevitably limited.

All these drawbacks are recognized, and much effort has been directed towards minimizing their effect, including substantial effort in the in-service training of careers teachers (INSET).

Trainers who have the opportunity and time to establish and maintain personal contacts with careers teachers in their areas will indirectly reap a harvest of recruits whose career choice is better informed. However, this is long-term work and it is important to bear in mind that direct recruiting from schools by employers is generally regarded as unacceptable, as it may unfairly limit pupils' choice and be discriminatory. It is expressly discouraged by the code of practice agreed between local education authorities and employers.

The compulsory school leaving age, after being raised progressively to 16, has generally ceased to be a battleground, although there are many who feel that all young people should receive vocational education or training up to the age of 18. In practice, the age of 16 is often a crux for occupational choice. The pupil is faced with four options:

1 a full-time academic course
2 a full-time vocational course
3 full-time employment (with or without further training or education)
4 the Youth Training scheme.

There has been much debate about the wisdom of the effects of the academic/vocational dichotomy. In a recent speech Peter Morgan,[3] Director General of the Institute of Directors, claimed that the educational élitism and the academic mould were important reasons for the under-performance of the UK economy. While many would not wholly agree with this view, there is fairly general agreement that a revision of attitudes, combined with broader-based courses, should be the aim.

Academic courses are most likely to be taken at school, and to be directed towards the A level examination, with the more distant objective of entry to higher education.

Within the public sector there is strong pressure to persuade as many pupils as possible to stay on into the sixth form, as the overall status of the school, its staff and financial factors will depend on the numbers doing so.

Vocational courses may be taken at school or at a college of further education. When aimed at qualifications, they may be those offered by BTEC, SCOTVEC, NVQs or a number of other bodies. Colleges of further education offer education provided after the conclusion of compulsory school attendance but not leading to a higher-ranked academic qualification. This has traditionally been the most direct link between the education system and career development. However, it is more usually a link between education and those who have already made a choice and entered their career, and for this reason is discussed in more detail in the next chapter.

The Certificate of Pre-vocational Education (CPVE), launched in 1985, offers young people who wish to continue at school after the compulsory leaving age but who are unsure of their objectives a course of practical, vocational and social skills leading to this recognized qualification. CPVE can be followed alongside A level programmes and through it students can acquire credits towards National Vocational Qualifications (see Chapter 8). Responsibility for the development of CPVE has, since the end of 1990, lain with City and Guilds.

The Technical and Vocational Education Initiative (TVEI) was established in 1984 by the Department of Employment, working through the then Manpower Services Commission (MSC), now the Training Enterprise and Educational Directorate (TEED). Originally a five-year experiment, it was extended into 1989 to cover all local education authorities. Its aims are to provide school pupils with a course combining general and pre-vocational education for pupils of all abilities in the 14–16 age range. The key element is seen to be practical, transferable skills in clusters closely related to industrial functions: manufacturing, marketing and the service area. Periods of work experience are an essential element.

The core elements of the TVEI curriculum are numeracy, communications, community studies, social and personal development (including careers) and outdoor pursuits. In practice, to the regret of some, TVEI has tended to be directed towards pupils of less than average ability or in the special needs category.

(The Youth Training Scheme and full-time employment are discussed in Chapter 4).

Higher education   Traditionally, the universities saw their role as carrying the torch of pure learning, rather than providing vocational training. In fact, the strength of the relationship between degree course and chosen vocation varies widely between disciplines. At one end of the scale, subjects such as law, architecture, mechanical engineering and medicine point clearly to an already chosen vocation, while, at the other, arts subjects such as English, history, classics and philosophy indicate no career choice.

Many university students choose subjects because they enjoy them, because they are good at them, or perhaps because they are able to get places to study them, rather than because they are the necessary foundation for a career. For this reason, they may not even consider career choice until towards the end of their final year.

The polytechnics were established in the 1960s, with the declared aim of providing higher vocational education, especially in technical areas. They were expected to foster close links with local industry and service it with suitably educated people. Some were felt to be slow to find their role, concentrating rather on copying the detached view of academic excellence held within universities. However, most have now found a valid place in the vocational development scene.

Universities and polytechnics have their own careers services. The expert, full-time staff of each are supported by visits from employers, especially during the 'milk round' (the annual recruiting visits by employers in the spring term) for final-year students. As with school pupils, however, such advice tends to be concentrated at a time when subject choices have long since been made and students are fully occupied preparing for exams.

Attendance on the milk round has usually been the preserve of larger employers seeking to recruit a number of graduates. It is expensive and time-consuming and, some would claim, inefficient. Some changes over recent years have helped. Group presentations in the autumn term (or even the second year) and careers fairs after final exams have spread the net wider and enhanced opportunities for communication, but this is still the almost exclusive preserve of big organizations.

Many employers regard the recruitment of graduates as a high-profile activity in which they are prepared to invest substantial sums. In those areas such as engineering where supply is lower than demand, the reason for this is clear. In others, it is difficult to restrain the feeling that there is an element of keeping up with Jones and Co plc—brochures become ever glossier and career promises, even if only implied, become ever wider. There has, for many years, been a danger of over-selling, which reaps a sad harvest in disillusionment in the first few years of employment for those recruited in this way.

The Careers Research and Advisory Centre (CRAC) runs four-day residential Insight programmes for undergraduates that offer them the opportunity to mix informally with younger managers from organizations active in graduate recruitment.

Industry/education links
For many years, the bridge between the worlds of education and work was the weakest point in initial career development.

While there are still problems, much attention has now been directed to the area and many initiatives have been taken. The rather bewildering growth of schemes includes some sponsored by national government, some by industry (collectively or by individual employers), some by the educational sector and some by specially established bodies (a selection of the more important is included under Useful organizations, pages 156–7).

These initiatives work by means of meetings, networks of personal contacts, literature, audio-visual and computer media. Some use business simulations, such as the computer-based competition for teams of sixthformers, 'Management Challenge', run annually by the British Institute of Management. Work shadowing (see Chapter 7) by pupils or teachers is used by some but the commonest technique is secondment (or 'attachment' as it may be called).

These schemes clearly contribute to career choice. Many employers regard participation in such schemes as virtually obligatory, but for success, commitment and much effort is essential. It is an area in which the skills and commitment of the professional trainer can make the difference between failure and success.

Experience of the 'world of work' for pupils still in full-time education is available in several ways:

- formally organized schemes of secondment
- part-time and vacation work
- sandwich courses.

Formally organized schemes of secondment (or attachment) are essential to the working of many of the industry/education links mentioned in the previous section.

Unfortunately, secondment is a technique that can be plagued with serious problems: the difficulty of giving meaningful work to the secondee in the time and with the resources available; of devoting sufficient time and attention to the secondee without disrupting other work; of debriefing and relating the experience to the everyday world of the secondee; and of finding people with the right skills and interests to guide, motivate and monitor the secondee. These are formidable difficulties that are rarely fully overcome. Also, the sheer number of would-be secondees makes the possibility of obtaining valid secondments increasingly difficult.

From the point of view of the employer and the training adviser, success in offering work experience relies on a number of ingredients:

- establishing direct, personal and preferably face-to-face contact with the teacher offering pupils for experience
- giving maximum information about your own organization before discussing individual secondments
- being frank and open about any difficulties that may arise from:
  —the nature of the work (is it uninteresting, complex, dirty, dangerous?)
  —the volume of work (is there too much, too little, is it irregular?)
  —personalities, whether management or shop floor
  —industrial relations aspects
- insisting on clear, sound learning objectives for each secondee being set and agreed before acceptance
- choosing the department or work area with great care

- setting up a system of mentoring (see Chapter 7) for each secondee
- ensuring that each secondee receives proper induction, including meaningful discussion with the appropriate manager and mentor
- ensuring regular meetings between secondee and mentor, monitoring their progress against set objectives
- conducting a concluding interview, also against set objectives
- providing a full report to the sponsoring teacher after secondment
- if regular secondment is planned, maintaining close, regular contact with the teachers involved.

Part-time and vacation work can be a factor in career choice for many young people. Such jobs may rarely be of the kind the pupil later chooses for their career as evening, morning, holiday and weekend jobs offer limited experience, but they have the overwhelming advantage of being real. The tasks are real, the relationships with colleagues and customers are real, the remuneration is real and the consequences of failure are real. Many see this as a better learning experience than artificially developed secondments.

The increasing flexibility of employment policy in many organizations is creating more and more opportunities like these. In some sectors, such as retailing and news agencies, regular part-time help from young people has become essential to the operation. If your organization has a work-load that peaks during holidays (with Christmas or Easter rushes, summer visitors and so on), vacation employment will be easy and economically sensible to arrange.

In every case, to maximize the career development value of part-time work requires a system of mentoring or regular, planned contact between student and professional.

Sandwich courses are educational courses typically at Higher National Diploma or degree level, during which substantial periods of time are spent gaining relevant experience with one or more employers. They are frequently used in engineering, computing and business studies courses.

'Thick' sandwiches take the form either of a first year with an employer, three academic years of study (often with industrial attachment during long vacations) and a final year of work experience, or a four-year course of which the third is spent on industrial attachment.

'Thin' sandwich courses frequently take the form of four-year courses split into six-month periods spent alternately in academic study and industrial experience. Government grants are available for industrial placements of not less than eight weeks in length by students following engineering, technology, computer science or similar courses.

Students on sandwich courses may be sponsored and paid during their industrial periods by one employer (company-based) or find the secondments necessary to complete their college course (college-based). The contract for company-based students is usually open from both sides; few employers attempt to insist that the student takes up full-time employment on completion and, equally, students have no right to such employment. However, in a high proportion of cases, both parties find themselves well satisfied and full-time employment with that company is the result.

Most educationalists and trainers agree that, when well-organized in appropriate subject areas, sandwich courses can form an ideal start for career development. The in-company periods of sandwich courses, especially when combined with financial sponsorship, are generally considered to be of great value. The professional skills of the trainer are essential to success in this as the trainer alone can ensure that the programme of work is well-structured, meaningful and closely related to the student's academic studies.

Formal sources of career advice

There are numerous sources of advice, some depending on the individual's position in (or out of) the education system. The roles of school careers teachers and the university and polytechnic careers services have already been mentioned, but others include:

- local education authority Careers Service
- private careers advisory services
- careers directories and other materials
- career fairs.

The LEA careers service

The Careers Service was founded early in this century as the Juvenile Employment Service with a remit to help all under the age of 18 or who were still at school. The Employment and Training Act 1973 abolished the age limit and laid a duty on local education authorities, under the oversight of the Department of Employment, to provide a vocational guidance service for those (with exceptions including universities and most evening and part-time classes) attending educational institutions. Careers Services can also keep in touch with young people who have left education and respond to their requests for careers help.

The main functions of the Service are:

- to work with careers and guidance teachers in schools and colleges in the careers education of young people and to provide them and their parents with information on educational, employment and training opportunities
- to give continuing vocational guidance to pupils and students in their later years at school or college and to help them reach informed and realistic decisions about their careers
- to help young people find suitable training and employment and employers to find suitable workers
- to offer help to young people with problems connected with their settlement in employment.[4]

The feeling is that, in some areas, the resources of the Service may be too limited to provide a meaningful service to individual students, particularly at school level. The traditional tension between school teachers and careers advisers has been mentioned above. Trainers will find that time and effort spent in establishing relationships with local careers advisers and supporting their work is worthwhile. They may also need to work 'smarter', rather than harder, in getting in touch with the real world of work.

Private careers advisory services
A number of private organizations offer advice on initial career choice. The process usually involves completion of a personal inventory, one or more interviews and the use of test instruments. Both the perceived value and cost of such services vary widely. Comments suggest that they may not often generate unexpected possibilities, although they can help in cases where the person is unsure about deciding on a particular career.

Careers directories and other materials
A wide range of materials aimed to help initial career choice is available from a number of sources. Among these are a number of publishers specializing in this area (see Bibliography, pages 159–60, for some useful titles).

The computer-based career choice aids include:

- the Careers Advisory Service Computer Aid (CASCAID), designed by the Leicestershire Careers Service
- the Job Ideas and Information Generator—Computer Assisted Learning (JIIG—CAL), designed by Edinburgh University business studies department and the London Borough of Havering
- the Educational Counselling and Credit Transfer Information Service (ECCTIS), designed by the Open University and privatized in September 1990.

Trainers may share with other members of the human resources function and managers the responsibility of ensuring that their organization is well represented in such publications. The increased volume of better-informed applicants usually amply justifies the effort. However, the temptation is to over-sell your organization. While it is unthinkable to present it in a bad light, it is more productive for both the organization and potential recruits to be specific, realistic and to avoid painting too glossy a picture, especially about opportunities for promotion.

Career fairs and open days
Career fairs and similar events are now frequently organized by schools and colleges or other organizations at which employers and bodies such as professional institutes are invited to set up a stand and be available to meet students and their parents to discuss career opportunities.

They offer a direct opportunity for employers to influence initial occupational choice. However, they vary widely in the clarity of their objectives and the efficiency of their organization. They also take time and require expertise (for example, the wrong choice of representatives can be counter-productive). Over-enthusiasm can be as damaging as lack of knowledge. However, most trainers who have attended would say that they feel that these events have contributed positively, both to individuals and to the general climate of opinion about the sector they represent.

To be of maximum value, representatives at career fairs should:

- be approachable and have a genuine interest in helping in the career development of young people
- be able to talk in language the enquirers will understand, but also be good listeners not over-fond of the sound of their own voice
- have a personal background that relates as closely as possible to that of the likely enquirers
- have sound, up-to-date general knowledge of the whole sector in which their organization operates
- know about the relevant qualifications and courses and how they relate to recruitment and employment in the sector
- be methodical and reliable in following up any promises made.

The employer's role

Employers have become steadily more involved in the processes of initial career choice, partly as a result of government policy and partly in self-defence. Most believe that this involvement is worthwhile, if not essential, the proportion responding as a matter of self-defence having grown substantially as the shortage of young recruits has become more marked.

'Industry' or 'the City' have in the past been allowed to become dirty words. Employers produce an effect in many ways, whether they plan to or not. As individuals, the more active and beneficial your role in the community, the more likely will young people be to listen to your advice and consider working for you. The more attractive the image of your profession—be it trainer, personnel officer, accountant, manager or whatever—the more likely it is to attract the interest of potential recruits. The better the image not only of your own organization but of the sector in which it belongs and, indeed, its broader categorization, the more it will attract the young.

The direct contributions employers can make to initial career choice have already been mentioned and include—they can visit schools and colleges, encourage visits to their own premises, organize open days, participate in career fairs, offer places for work experience schemes, make available part-time and vacation jobs for young people and can become school governors—but there are others, too.

The recruitment advertising policy of the organization will also have its influence. The way opportunities are presented will not only affect the filling of the specific vacancies, but will contribute, for better or worse, to the climate of opinion in which their organization, their sector of the economy and even economic activity as a whole is viewed by young people.

Action check-list
- Give our own children the best career advice.
- Contribute to the media on careers subjects.
- Join boards of school governors and parent-teacher associations.
- Donate needed equipment and provide technical support for schools.
- Participate in schemes linking education and the world of work.
- Offer and support actively secondments for school pupils and teachers.
- Consider and, if chosen, support actively the use of company- or college-based sandwich courses for initial recruitment of skilled people.
- Establish contact with the local Careers Service.
- Provide good material for career directories.
- Attend career fairs and open days.

References
1. French, Dr Jane, *The Education of Girls—A Handbook for Parents* (Cassell, 1990).
2. MORI survey for Reader's Digest, reported by Will Bennett in the *Independent*, 26 September, 1990.
3. Morgan, Peter, in a paper to a BTEC seminar, reported by Ngaio Crequer in the *Independent*, 19 September, 1990.
4. 'The work of the Careers Service'. Official Report published by the Department of Employment and the Welsh and Scottish Offices, 1981.

3 Recruitment

The act of recruitment is on the critical path of career development so mistakes are likely to have far-reaching effects. For the sake both of individual and employer, it must be seen as a two-way process: the penalties for error are great for both. There are many tools to help selection but none is exact and all need careful choice and skilled use. A number of outside agencies are available to help.

The trainer has a key role in this process—frequently having the opportunity to train managers in selection interviewing—so should take every opportunity to extend this brief to the complete recruitment process, of which interviewing is only one component.

The selection situation

For employers, choosing the best people to fill their job vacancies is important. The more important the post, the more critical the choice. Finding the right chief executive, the right technologist or the right craftsman, for example, may make the difference between success and failure for the organization.

The same is true for individuals. Choosing the right employer may prove critical to the career and so, compared with this, many other aspects of career development pale into insignificance.

The penalties for error

For the employer, the penalties of selecting a poor candidate include low efficiency, damage and waste of materials, upset customers or clients, harm to interpersonal relationships among colleagues and loss of confidence in those responsible for the choice. To these must be added the often substantial costs of recruitment and re-recruitment and the learning curve of a replacement employee.

The cost of failing to pick the right candidate can be even greater. The organization will lose this person's services, while another, possibly a competitor, will retain or gain them. For a top-level post, such an error may be fatal.

For the individual the penalties are also high. Choosing to accept the wrong post can result in lack of job satisfaction, frustration, stress, mental and physical ill-health, family problems, (especially if relocation is involved), financial loss, long-term damage to career prospects, pressure to find another post, which may produce a further mistake—possibly unemployment.

Failure to recognize a good opportunity will result in long-term, possibly irreparable, damage to the career. As Shakespeare pointed out, ideal opportunities rarely come round a second time.

The two-way process Matching individuals to jobs must be a two-way process in which applicant and employer are equal partners. While the initiative to offer or not to offer lies with the employer, both parties must, for success, make their own judgement about the situation and both need sufficient information and every available aid in making that judgement.

The requirements are, in theory, simple. The employer must have:

- a clear idea of the job vacancy—usually embodied in a job description
- thought carefully about the sort of characteristics needed in the person who is to fill this job, embodying them in a person profile
- decided what remuneration is feasible and what the other conditions of employment are to be.

The applicant must have:

- knowledge of their own skills, expertise, career aims and failings
- learnt as much as possible in advance about the recruiting organization and the job applied for
- decided what minimum remuneration and other conditions of employment are acceptable.

Each armed with their knowledge, the two must exchange as much relevant information as possible. In doing so, they must tell the truth, the whole truth and nothing but the truth. They must then help each other towards a decision and negotiate a mutually acceptable outcome.

The need for full disclosure suggests that a third party may often help the process as an honest broker. Skilled selection consultants can perform this role well (see pages 34–5).

The problems of selection

Selection is always an attempt to achieve the almost impossible—to predict human behaviour. It is not surprising, then, that there are many soft spots in the selection process—some psychological, some technical.

Pressures on the employer There are many pressures on the employer. The employer will:

- be aware that he or she alone can make or withhold a job offer and this may produce a false sense of power which obscures the fact that the process is two-way and depends for its success on the most complete mutual exchange of information
- naturally wish to present the organization in the best light and will be tempted to over-sell both it and the job
- feel, like most people, that he or she can judge others accurately and be reluctant to accept that, especially within the constraints of recruitment, it is an extremely difficult task

- sometimes relegate recruitment a low priority and fail to read documents or complete the other necessary preparation properly and in good time
- be prone, when a number of people are involved in the decision, to interpersonal, political or status difficulties that make good selection harder
- feel strong pressure to make what may later prove an unsuitable appointment if there is a shortage of apparently suitable applicants.

The use of a sound system for recruitment and the training of all involved in its use is the best hedge against such pressures. The establishment of the system is a key human resources development role and the elements it must contain are discussed below. Training in the use of the system is a responsibility for which the trainer should be pro-active. Few managers are prepared to give recruitment and selection the time it requires, and even fewer have the humility to accept their need for training.

Pressures on the candidate

The candidate also feels many pressures, including having:

- no clear career plans
- failed to define the objectives for the job choice
- imperfect insight into his or her strengths and weaknesses
- not read or understood the details of what is on offer
- a real need for *any* job, because he or she is unemployed, has financial problems or is very unhappy in a present job
- to deal with the competitiveness of the situation, which could spur the person towards a degree of deceit, varying from being economical with the truth to downright lying
- a wish to gain a job offer as a symbol of success, whether the job is suitable or not.

The recruitment system

The selection tools may be chosen or used badly or they may be relied upon too much for support. This is especially true of the interview.

Some selectors use only a limited range of recruitment tools, either from habit or lack of knowledge of what is available. Many are unaware of the limitations of those that they do choose. Frequently those involved have received little or no training.

The elements in a sound system include:

- the job description
- the person profile
- advertisements
- application forms and c.v.s
- references
- interviews
- tests and examinations—aptitude, intelligence and personality tests
- group tasks

- handwriting analysis
- assessment centres.

Astrology and nepotism are not unknown components of some systems.

The job description

A systematic written description of each post is now almost universally used, except in some of the smallest and newest organizations. Such descriptions will include the following information:

- job title
- department
- grade or salary range
- the key purpose of the post
- who the holder reports to
- the duties and responsibilities
- for whom the holder is responsible
- necessary relationships with other departments/posts
- any external relationships.

Job descriptions are the essential basis for systematic recruitment, but are not always as helpful as they could be. They can be stilted, limiting and unrealistic. They can rapidly get out of date. It is essential that they should be checked and, if necessary, revised before the process goes any further. A sample job description is shown in Figure 3.1.

The person profile

The person profile (sometimes called the person specification) is often the missing link in the selection process. Having defined the job to be filled in the job description, it is necessary to define the characteristics of the person we would like to fill it.

It is useful to divide these into 'musts' (criteria against which we are not prepared to compromise) and 'wants' (criteria against which we can compare candidates who pass the musts).

However, no criteria should be designated as a must unless there is a valid reason. The qualifications and experience required may be too tightly defined—qualifications and experience are not ends in them-selves but only possible predictors of future performance. Many good candidates are rejected out of hand and many careers spoilt by limit-ations of this kind that are unnecessarily arbitrary.

Musts, even if only implied, can be abused to discriminate unfairly. They can, for example, have sexual overtones, 'Be of a caring disposi-tion', 'should be fully mobile', 'be capable of heavy lifting' may each be justified but may also each be misused. Age limits are also frequently arbitrary and unjustified. 'Ageism' is a form of career-destroying dis-crimination that is already illegal in some countries.

Many frequently used want criteria are unhelpful if not completely meaningless. Virtually every person profile will be found to include such wants as 'good communicator', 'good interpersonal skills', 'com-mitted and conscientious', but such criteria have minimal value as a means of selection.

Job title   Organization and Methods and Information Systems Manager

Key purpose   To ensure that the organization, methods of use of information and other indirect work meet the needs of the company efficiently and effectively.

Reporting to   The Director of Financial Services

Grade   Management staff grade five

Duties and responsibilities

- To provide a service for the evaluation and improvement of all systems of indirect (i.e., non-production) work and the obtaining, recording and use of information within the company.
- To provide a service for the measurement of the volume of work in any indirect work area and to assess the skills and numbers necessary to complete it.
- To advise management as required on the establishment of methods and systems for indirect work and all aspects of information systems and technology.
- To advise management as required on the most suitable and cost-effective machinery, equipment or other facilities for indirect work including all information systems.
- To manage those reporting to him directly and indirectly.
- To meet the budgetary and other targets set for his area.
- To undertake such other duties as the directors may require.

Staff reporting

- Three O&M and IS Team Leaders
- The Information and Office Technology Adviser
- The Leader of the Indirect Work Measurement team
- The Operations Research and Statistics Adviser

Relationships

The O&M Manager must establish and maintain good relationships with all departmental managers and others necessary for the successful undertaking of his or her responsibilities; must maintain good working contacts with suppliers of machinery, equipment and other facilities for the information handling and other non-production work required for the efficient operation of the company.

Figure 3.1   Sample job description

It may be useful, however, to specify *negative* criteria—aspects that would lessen a candidate's appeal (negative wants), or rule them out of consideration (negative musts).

Person profiles have a tendency to end up as defining an unattainable paragon—someone fit only for the chief executive's chair. We must be realistic and avoid over-specifying.

An example of a person profile for the post in the sample job description shown in Figure 3.1 is given in Figure 3.2.

> **Title of post**   Organization and Methods and Information Systems Manager
>
> **Must**
>
> - Have degree or equivalent.
> - Have at least five years' directly relevant experience.
> - Be prepared to travel throughout Europe.
>
> **Want**   *Weight*
>
> - Ability to persuade and produce change.   10
> - Clear and challenging thinker.   10
> - Effective manager of professional staff.   10
> - Experience of computing and other aspects of IT.   9
> - Up-to-date knowledge of information systems and technology.   9
> - Experience of the measurement of indirect work.   6

Figure 3.2   Sample person profile

Advertisements   Effective advertising plays an important role in the matching of people to jobs available by helping candidates to undertake rational self-selection. The aim will be to attract a small field of the most suitable candidates. As with all advertising, however, there is a danger of deliberate or unintentional over-selling as many organizations see recruitment advertising as contributing to their image. It certainly does this, but, in the long run, those individuals whose hopes have been raised falsely, whose time has been wasted and, at worst, who have ended up in unsuitable jobs will harm the image more than any immediate impact of the advertisement. The wording and placing of the advertisement must, therefore, give as much accurate information in the space available as possible.

An example of a job advertisement for the post given in the sample job description in Figure 3.1 is shown in Figure 3.3.

Application forms and c.v.s   Many application forms are badly designed. While the application form will become part of the contract between employer and successful candidate, it should also be of help in the selection process by providing evidence against the criteria on the person profile. If it indicates whether the musts are met, it will help to decide whether to call the candidate for interview.

If candidates provide a c.v., it is unnecessary and ill-mannered to insist on completion of an application form before interview, even though it may be required for contractual reasons at a later stage. Many candidates now have c.v.s professionally prepared, and it is increasingly necessary, therefore, to judge them by their factual content rather than the quality of presentation.

References   The taking up of references is usually felt to be of value, although much depends on how it is done. Many recruiters feel that telephone (or face-

The XYZ Company wishes to recruit an

ORGANIZATION AND METHODS AND INFORMATION SYSTEMS MANAGER

based at its headquarters in Corby, Northamptonshire.

The Company produces a range of plastic gnomes and leprechauns in its UK, French and Eire plants that are sold throughout Europe. It has a work-force of 5500 and employs state-of-the-art technology, both for manufacturing and indirect work. Founded in 1979, it has expanded steadily to its present size and is now generally regarded as one of the European market leaders.

The O&M and IS Manager will report to the Director of Financial Services. He or she will be responsible for ensuring that the organization, methods of use of information and other indirect work meet the needs of the company efficiently and effectively. The Manager will control a team of 35 staff, many of degree level, working in the areas of information technology and organization and methods. He or she must have a good degree-level qualification, at least five years' relevant experience and be prepared to travel throughout Europe. The abilities to think clearly, challenge established practices and produce change are paramount.

The Company operates an equal opportunities policy and welcomes applications from disabled people.

An attractive remuneration package will be offered to the successful applicant.

Please apply, with full c.v., to Ms P. R. Sonnel, XYZ Company, Corby, Northamptonshire.

Figure 3.3 Sample job advertisement

to-face) discussions with referees are more useful than written references, which tend to be bland and require skilled interpretation—usually based on what they *do not* say rather than what they say!

Interviews   The selection interview presents a nearly insoluble contradiction. On the one hand, numerous studies have shown that its value is hardly greater than tossing a coin, but, on the other hand, to fill a vacancy without interviewing the candidates for it is unthinkable.

Interviewing is a complex skill in which improvement calls for humility, training and practise. Common problems include:

- lack of preparation
- failure to follow a systematic process to gain evidence for the criteria on the person profile
- failure to establish a rapport as soon as possible

- premature judgement, often within the first few seconds
- irrational biases based on sex, age, appearance or dress
- poor questioning technique, including the use of leading questions
- failure to listen actively and accurately
- failure to read body language
- failure to probe doubts fully
- failure to check understanding
- over-emphasis on the candidate's career misjudgements, such as a wrong initial choice of career or job
- desire by the interviewer for flattery and confirmation of their opinions
- use of meaningless favourite or trick questions
- failure to give sufficient or accurate information to candidates.

Training in interviewing is most effective when it includes practise interviews that are videoed and played back. Playback can be organized in several ways. Groups of three (interviewer, interviewee and observer) working together offer the opportunity for more thorough feedback and lessen the fear of exposure. The observer role in such groups is often of particular value.

Many trainers obtain the services of 'real life' interviewees (say, pupils or students), thus achieving the extra benefit of giving them practise in being interviewed.

The interview series   A series of interviews can be set up in many different ways.

It is helpful when interviews are combined with a completely informal opportunity for the candidate to meet some of those who would be colleagues if the application proves successful, or who have held the job for which the candidate has applied. Such a meeting will usually provide both candidate and employer with a goldmine of useful data that will make the subsequent interview or interviews far more useful.

It is also helpful to involve more than one person in the selection process. This lessens the risk of bias and preconception and the extent to which the 'chemistry' between individuals affects the decision. Candidates who fail with one interviewer may shine with another and both can provide evidence towards the final decision.

The use of more than one interview is also helpful. Frequently a first interview will be used as a tool for building up a short list, followed by a second, sometimes even a third interview as the number of candidates is reduced. An advantage of a two-stage process is that the first interview can be conducted on an informal one-to-one basis, facilitating the building of a close rapport and the exchange of information.

Panels are usually used at the second or final stage of the process in order to allow several people to meet the candidate and pool impressions. The larger the panel, the more formal and less effective the interview will inevitably be (four is a sensible maximum). A panel should meet in advance (unless it frequently interviews together) to plan tactics and learn as much as possible about each other's style. Evaluation can cause problems for a panel, so it is helpful to agree on the process before starting the interviews. Methodical use of the person profile is particularly important for panel interviewing to ensure that all criteria are covered at interview and as a basis for the subsequent evaluation.

Tests and examinations

Tests or examinations can add to the information about the candidate provided by their qualifications, experience and interview performance. If the person profile calls for specific knowledge or skill, we may be able to find or devise a test for it. However, the choice and use of tests needs careful consideration. There are many different kinds with varying relevance and validity in different situations and we must be clear as to what a test can do. In some cases a test can only provide raw material for later exploration or confirm (or cast doubt on) other evidence.

Performance tests

The performance test is used to assess a skill directly needed in the job. Thus, a shorthand typist can be given a shorthand test or an HGV driver may be asked to demonstrate skills in manoeuvring a long vehicle in a confined space. If properly devised and conducted, tests of this sort can be invaluable.

Written examinations

These may have the same function as performance tests when the post requires specific knowledge—a geography test for a post with a travel agent, for example.

Aptitude tests

These are of value when selecting those without previous experience in a particular kind of work. They are predictive in that they set out to forecast how an individual can perform in a future situation. This is based on a demonstrable link between performance in the test and later job performance, possibly after training. Such tests are well established in the selection process for a wide range of jobs, including computer programmers, systems analysts, pilots and many others.

Intelligence tests

Intelligence tests seek to measure a person's intelligence quotient (IQ), which is seen as a measure of general mental ability capable of application to a wide range of tasks and situations. They are often sub-divided into verbal, numerical and spatial abilities. IQ tests have been used in selection for many years. However, as with personality tests (see below), most employers lack data correlating test results with actual job performance and their use is probably now declining.

Personality tests

Personality tests have an irresistible fascination for some people. Most are designed to provide a personality profile based on specific dimensions. They must, by definition, be based on a particular view of the human personality and its operation—a subject on which there is only limited agreement.

A massive range of such tests now exists, from the Luscher Colour Test, which aims to assess aspects of personality from the order in which eight colours are ranked, to the Minnesota Multiphrasic Personality

Inventory (MMPI) Test, which takes several hours to administer and mark and depends upon reactions to several hundred statements on cards. Other tests, such as the Myers-Briggs Type Indicator (MBTI), Sixteen Personality Factor Questionnaire (16PF) and Occupational Personality Questionnaire (OPQ) have been found useful by a large number of organizations—as one source of information about an applicant. Most tests are copyright and so can only be bought and used by those licensed to do so, usually after training by the copyright holder.

Probably the most serious danger in the use of personality tests for selection is the logical gap that often exists between test result and job performance. It is tempting to interpret test results subjectively, but, 'Good salespeople must be extroverts, this test shows A is extrovert, A will therefore succeed as a salesperson' is, at best, risky logic. What evidence do we have for the belief that good salespeople *must* be extroverts? Have salespeople been measured on this dimension? If so, how similar was the job context of those measured to the job context in which A is expected to operate? How was 'success' measured and how applicable is this measure to our particular requirements? Research in this area is taking place and one day we might have some answers.

Few tests will have been validated in conditions sufficiently close to our own. The process of validation may require sample sizes that we cannot attain. It may require accurate measures of job success that do not exist, particularly in professional and managerial jobs. Collecting validating data may often involve testing existing jobholders who have been in their posts sufficiently long for success to be meaningfully measured.

Some feel that the concept of personality testing is intrusive and dangerous and that, wrongly used, they create a feeling of spurious accuracy. Those supporting the use of tests will claim that their use is entirely proper, given safeguards. These should include:

- only administering tests on individuals who have been briefed on the purpose of the test
- obtaining prior agreement of the individual to be tested
- careful and proper administration of the tests
- sharing the test results with individuals tested
- maintaining full confidentiality for all results in both the short and long term
- proper and fully controlled use of the test results.

Group tasks Group tasks are frequently used as a tool for selection for posts in which interpersonal skills are important. Tests in which a group has to accomplish a physical task (such as transporting a burden over an obstacle) have been used since the Second World War by War Office Selection Boards (WOSBs) for officer selection in the British army.

Group discussions have also established a place in a number of selection procedures for posts in which related skills are needed.

Handwriting analysis

Many people now feel this technique must be taken seriously. It is extensively used in Europe and so seems likely to become commoner in the UK. Its value and reliability, however, are areas of discussion and most British human resources professionals probably regard it as still unproven. Handwriting analysis shares the same problems as psychometric testing in that even if its predictive value for elements of behaviour can be satisfactorily demonstrated, most employers lack adequate, objective data linking this to successful job performance.

Assessment centres

Assessment centres (see Chapter 11) are more commonly used for the assessment of existing staff. However, when a number of people are being matched at the same time for the same vacancies (as with an annual intake of graduates), assessment centres can be both efficient and economical. Probably the original and oldest assessment centres in the UK are the WOSBs mentioned above and those used for selection to senior Civil Service grades.

The role of agencies, consultants, head-hunters and Jobcentres

There are several external agencies available to help in matching people to jobs: Jobcentres, employment agencies, selection consultants and 'head-hunters'.

Jobcentres

The government-run Jobcentres (successors to Employment Exchanges) operate by accepting and advertising vacancies from employers, conducting preliminary interviews of those seeking employment and passing on their details to the employer. They are concerned mainly with less skilled jobs. They do not undertake detailed matching or selection.

Employment agencies

Employment agencies aim to attract job-seekers who they can recommend to employers either for specific vacancies of which they have been notified, or against long-term or recurring needs. They will keep registers of those looking for work and are frequently pro-active in approaching employers. Most agencies retain staff to fill employers' temporary vacancies. Agencies usually specialize in a particular area such as secretarial, computer or accounting staff.

Agencies can help individuals seeking jobs by providing a wider field of choice and setting up the first contact with potential employers. They are the only practicable source of help for those who want temporary work. However, few agencies are stringent in their vetting either of employers or applicants. Some have also acquired a reputation for very hard selling.

Selection consultants

Selection consultants help client organizations to fill a vacancy by accepting a brief, advising on salary level and other matters, writing and placing an advertisement, accepting and sifting applications, conducting first interviews and presenting a fully documented short list to the client for final choice. They normally work in the area of middle and senior management and professional jobs, and are sometimes confused with 'head-hunters' (see below).

Selection consultants can be of particular help to smaller organizations without a large human resource development function or when filling unusual or specialized vacancies. They can help organizations of any size by undertaking part of what can be burdensome and resource-consuming process.

Both selection and search consultants see their role as that of an 'honest broker', if only because their fee payment will depend largely on making a successful placement. They will therefore offer candidates as much information as possible about the vacancy and the client in order to maximize the chances of success, even to the extent of indicating potential problem areas or personalities. For this reason, they can often be of more help to candidates—and thus indirectly to employers—than a direct application to an employer.

The use of consultants also enables organizations that wish to do so to remain anonymous until a late stage in the process.

Head-hunters

Executive search consultants—commonly called head-hunters—usually operate only at the highest level. After receiving a brief, they will approach individuals who may be interested personally and privately, conducting initial discussions up to the point where sufficient serious interest has been detected to justify setting up direct contact between potential candidate and employer.

As Michael Dixon of the *Financial Times* has said,[1] it is arguable that snobbery has overtaken effectiveness in this field. The true role of search consultants should be to locate and approach those possessing rare skills needed by their client at whatever level—whether chief executives or multilingual craftsmen—for whom a wide, general trawl would be neither efficient nor cost effective.

Codes of conduct

Several codes of conduct have been drawn up to cover the process of external recruitment. Most notable of these is the code first issued by the Institute of Personnel Management (IPM) in 1978,[2] which

. . . seeks to promote high standards of professional recruitment practice by encouraging recruiters and applicants to adhere to common guidelines.

The guidelines cover such areas as handling unsolicited applications, interviewees' expenses, taking up references and discrimination and define the obligations of both recruiters and applicants.

Other codes of conduct in recruitment include the code for the recruitment of graduates, produced by the Association of Recruiters of

Graduates (ARG) and the Association of Graduate Careers and Advisory Services (AGCAS).

Action check-list

- Encourage all concerned to see recruitment as a two-way process.
- Train recruiters to produce and use good person profiles.
- Warn recruiters against over-selling vacancies in advertisements or at interview.
- Train managers to choose from and use effectively the complete range of selection tools.
- Train all concerned in the techniques of effective selection interviewing.
- Ensure that tests are only used in appropriate, controlled situations with stringent validation of results.
- Encourage the use of selection consultants in appropriate circumstances.
- Inform recruiters about the IPM and other recruitment codes of conduct and encourage their observance.

References

1. Dixon, Michael, 'Time to Cut Head-hunting Down to Size', the *Financial Times*, 27 June, 1990.
2. *The IPM Recruitment Code* (Institute of Personnel Management, 1988).

4 The first job

The transition from full-time education to first employment can be the most critical and difficult stage of career development—what happens then can affect the individual's attitudes to work, employment and their career deeply and permanently. It gains immensely if the job experience is combined with further vocational education and training; good apprenticeships and traineeships are ideal. Whatever else happens, there must be an effective induction programme and continuing support from the individual's manager, human resources professionals and any relevant professional institutions.

The training professional is deeply and directly involved during this phase, being involved in induction programme design and aspects of their presentation, designing and participating in running apprenticeships and traineeships, assisting in developing managers' awareness of and skills in handling their responsibilities to the new starter and maybe acting as a coach or mentor.

The transition to employment

This is the most critical career phase of all. As with the early days of childhood, mistakes here tend to last a lifetime and be almost impossible to correct. This transition will set the pattern for the individual's subsequent career development: the individual who feels neglected, who receives no adequate guidance and support or who is not developed positively during this phase will lose opportunities and gain attitudes that may stunt and poison the rest of their career.

It is not only in the interest of the individual and the employer to provide the best skill development during this phase but also of the country. If the opportunities it presents are lost, the whole economic system is damaged, as has been recognized in a string of legislation over the past 30 years, but there are problems. Because many of the skills gained during this phase are transferable, some employers are reluctant to risk providing trained manpower for their competitors. Some smaller organizations lack or feel they lack, the resources to train and openly rely on attracting people trained by larger, training-conscious organizations, but organizations that do not bear their share of training have only themselves to blame in times of skill shortage.

The training legislation of the sixties and seventies was designed to encourage all to train, thus spreading the cost more fairly. The direct financial incentives of the Industrial Training Board levy/grant system are no longer in place, but the locally-based Training and Education Councils (TECs) have been established to address the same problem (they are discussed in Chapter 8).

It is no longer sensible to concentrate training on those individuals judged to have greatest potential at the expense of the rest. The proportion of unskilled jobs is growing rapidly less and today's knowledge-based economy requires the fullest development of the potential of *all*. The need for vocational development is as great whether the start is made at the age of 21–23 into a professional career or 16. Indeed, those who fail initially to gain employment may, arguably, be said to have the greatest need of all, because, not only have they lost out as individuals, but society has lost the economic contribution they could make.

Everyone involved in the development process—managers and supervisors, trainers and providers of further education—will need to deploy their best skills during this phase. All the tools of development are needed, together with a number of special aids.

A good induction programme will be essential for all. For some, an apprenticeship or extended traineeship will be appropriate. Those who have found difficulty in gaining employment will need the support of a government-sponsored scheme such as Youth Training. Those who have left school at 16 will benefit from further education, as may many who have left later. The organization may find benefit in sponsoring students on sandwich courses. The recruitment of graduates will call for careful thought. Those aiming for a profession will need the continuing support of their professional institute. For all, their first job experience itself will be critical.

Induction training

For the individual at the start of a career, the effectiveness of initial induction will have a deep and long-lasting effect on attitude to work and employment.

Induction training is aimed at introducing new employees to the organization, its products (or services), its structure, personnel and method of working and to their own role in it. It helps them to learn their job more rapidly and contribute as soon as possible, shows them how their role fits with others in the organization, teaches safe practices for themselves and others and contributes to long-term efficiency and motivation.

Effective induction will include:

- an extended meeting with the direct manager or supervisor
- introductions to all individuals who will be in direct contact with the jobholder
- explanation of all safety rules, supported by any necessary documentation
- housekeeping information—the layout of the work area, car parking or travel arrangements, canteen, washrooms

- discussion of the main terms and conditions of employment, including hours of work, sickness, holidays, expenses and payment, including overtime
- full information on the duties and responsibilities of the work
- training and supervised practise in all necessary skills.

An induction package is a frequent component in the process. However, its use must never become a substitute for the many face-to-face elements; it should be regarded only as a means of reinforcing the oral communication and providing a record for future reference. It should be written simply (but not in a patronizing style) and laid out in a clear, open format. A question-and-answer approach may be suitable. To include complex and lengthy instructions, legal documents or brochures produced for other purposes (such as selling) is counter-productive. Training professionals are often particularly well placed to produce such packages. An example of an outline for an induction package is given in Figure 4.1.

The timing of the elements of induction is important. There is a danger of leaving elements too late, or introducing them too early; of crowding trainees, or leaving them too long to their own devices. The overall length of induction will vary between a few hours and many days, with those starting their career being likely to need longer than those moving between jobs. It may be either on- or off-the-job or both. A modular structure is frequently helpful and if the programme is of any complexity or length, it is usually best to intersperse all but the first stage with periods of on-the-job work. In some cases, the trainees themselves may be asked to suggest when they feel ready to move to the next element.

When employees are recruited from outside in batches or large numbers, it may be helpful to carry out some of the induction process in a group. However, this is not a substitute for those essential elements involving the departmental manager and the job-specific skills and knowledge.

Induction is, of course, necessary for those moving to new jobs within the organization as well as those recruited from outside. It is a trap to assume that existing employees know all they need to, particularly with regard to the roles of their new job, new colleagues and, if it is the case, new department.

As with other types of training, the manager cannot be allowed to duck out and leave induction to others. Apart from working together on the setting of training objectives and ensuring that both content and method are right, the manager will need to play a part in the process personally in order to start building the personal relationship with the new starter so vital to subsequent development. He or she may also help to produce the induction package described above. The training professional will need to direct at least as much attention to the manager as to the new employee.

Welcome to the recruit
Maybe a short, personalized letter from the chief executive, including recruit's name, department, job title, name of supervisor or manager and name of contact within the human resources department.

Basic facts about the organization
What it does, makes, etc.
Outline history.
Size: number of employees, turnover, number of sites, etc.
Ownership, links with other organizations, statutory position, etc., as appropriate.

The recruit's department/work area
Location.
Manager.
Outline organization structure.
Purpose.
Working relationships, internal and external.

The recruit's job
Job description.
Reference to supervisor/manager and other sources of help.

Housekeeping
The layout of the work area.
Car parking or travel arrangements.
Canteen.
Washrooms, etc.

Safety
Statement of safety policy.
Outline of dangers of job.
Basic safety precautions/rules.

Training
Description of induction programme.
Other training arrangements.
Appraisal procedure and purpose.

Basic conditions of employment
Job title.
Remuneration, including date and method of payment or overtime, bonuses, etc.
Hours of work.
Period of notice.
Sickness arrangements.
Probationary period.
Leave entitlement and arrangements.
Disciplinary procedure.
Reference to full contract of employment and sources of further information.

Figure 4.1 *An example of an outline for an induction package*

Apprenticeships and traineeships

Apprenticeships are the oldest form of industrial training—indeed, for many centuries they were the *only* form. The earliest references to apprenticeship in England go back about 600 years.

The formal apprenticeship involved the establishment of a contract or 'indenture' between the learner (the apprentice) and the craftsman for a fixed term of years. The apprentice was 'bound' by this to learn, obey and work as instructed; the master to teach the mysteries of the craft. The craft guilds would allow craft status only to those who had successfully completed their indentures. Some professional training followed a similar pattern; the legal profession had, as long ago as 1400, a system of pupillage under which pupils paid fees for the privilege of shadowing experienced barristers.

The indenture could cover almost any aspect of behaviour and discipline, including the place of residence of the apprentice. The apprenticeship was thus firmly based on the concept of *total* development: knowledge, skill and personality combined in achieving job competence. However, the *quality* of development depended heavily on the ability and commitment of the master. There was no provision for off-the-job education and virtually no way of opting out of the contract.

Apprenticeship, of up to seven years in length, gradually became a prerequisite for many careers, ranging from skilled manual trades to (under a different name) professions such as accountancy and the law. Today, the initial period of craft apprenticeship is usually spent under full-time instruction in an apprentice training school. Organizations with a large annual intake of apprentices have established their own schools, in many cases with excellent facilities and highly skilled staff. Smaller organizations have made use of groups schemes or the facilities of a local college. After completion of the basic training, elements of study by day or block release for an appropriate qualification are combined with supervised practical work and additional shorter periods of off-the-job instruction. The quality of an apprenticeship now depends far less on the character of individual craftsmen, and is supported by trained instructors and teachers. In recent years, the making of formal indentures has been replaced by variations of standard conditions of employment.

Apprenticeships were, for many years, the backbone of industrial and professional training and regarded by many as providing an excellent mix of learning, skill and personal development. In recent years, however, they have suffered a major eclipse and the size of intakes has plummeted. There are a number of reasons for this.

For the employer, the recruitment of regular intakes of apprentices requires anticipation of the need for trained manpower up to six years ahead. Such a planning horizon presents problems for organizations of any size, especially in periods of rapid change, and may be impossible for smaller firms. Inevitably in times of financial stringency, such as the early eighties, intakes of apprentices have been the first area for cost cutting, however irrational or short-sighted this may later seem to have been.

Apprenticeships have also been an important element in the maintenance of lines of demarcation and inflexibility between skilled trades. Union pressure on apprentices' wages has made the employment of large numbers of apprentices costly. They have been increasingly perceived as more a mechanism for maintaining the scarcity value of craft skills than an effective method of development.

For the individual, the rigid age-limits for apprenticeships have become increasingly restrictive as educational patterns have become more flexible. The length of traditional apprenticeships has also made them less attractive than the higher wages immediately available from unskilled jobs.

Despite these negative aspects, *good* apprenticeships have much to recommend them. For the individual, they provide a sound base for development; a demonstrable level of skill and knowledge that can be transferred, if necessary, to other contexts and other employers. Within larger organizations, apprenticeships have offered a superb developmental ladder, with the best of those who begin at craft level being given the opportunity to move on to technician level, some even progressing to HND or graduate courses. For the organization, apprenticeships provide a hallmark of skill, develop loyalty and implant the organization's own working practices and philosophy.

Apprenticeships have been dragged down by their own history, perceived as being inextricably linked with heavy industry and the restrictive and inflexible use of labour. This seems a pity, as, seen in another light, they could have formed the model for a wide range of training. In many areas, apprenticeships have been replaced by the use of Youth Training. Shorter, progressively structured and monitored apprenticeships are still felt to have a role in the development of craft skills, but their decline has left a gap in skills development that has only partly been filled.

Youth training

The dual needs for a well-trained work-force and a reduction in the numbers of unemployed 16–19-year-olds have combined to produce a succession of political initiatives. Youth Training (YT) is the current successor to the Youth Opportunities Programmes (YOP) and the Youth Training Scheme (YTS).

YT offers 48 weeks of employer-based education and training with an allowance and what is described as '. . . a 40–60 per cent chance of a full-time job on completion'. Of the time, 13 weeks are spent in relevant education in literacy, numeracy, manual dexterity, computer literacy and IT, life and social skills. Most trainees are employer-based, although there is provision for basing them in colleges of further education or voluntary schemes. The training is designed and the placements administered on behalf of the TEED by approved managing agents, who may be employers, colleges, local authorities or private consultants. The laid-down allowance for trainees is partly subsidized and partly paid by the employer. Performance is continuously assessed, individual profiles are completed, and a certificate is issued. Employers are free to employ or not to employ the trainees on completion of their training.

The scheme has tended to replace traditional apprenticeships or other forms of training in some fields, such as hairdressing. It has become more attractive to some employers as a means of recruitment as the available numbers of young people have dropped.

Sadly this has proved to be a highly political area, bedevilled by charge and counter-charge. Attempts have been made to tie payment of social security benefits to participation in such training, and there are suggestions of full compulsion. Some trade unions feel that such schemes are regarded by employers as a source of cheap labour or as a means of diluting traditional craft training. Some individuals and some employers see such attempts as an irrelevant burden.

Professional trainers have formed varying views about the value of YT, but many have concluded that, with their active support and that of their organizations, it can provide the basis for excellent initial skills development for many young people.

Vocational education and training for 16–18-year-olds

There are currently strong pressures to provide continuing vocational education and training to all 16–18-year-olds in employment, whether linked to YT, apprenticeships or not. It is generally felt that the UK lags behind other industrialized countries in this area and that its economic performance will suffer—may already have suffered—from this deficiency. Suggestions have been made that all employers should be required to provide a guaranteed minimum degree of support. The means suggested for achieving this include generous day or block release, a number of days' educational leave per year, vouchers that can be spent on education or training of the individual's own choice, or in-house provision by the employer.

Resistance has come from both individuals and employers. Individuals may feel no interest in education and be glad to have escaped from a system they disliked, so compulsion is particularly unlikely to be successful for this age group. Employers may be anxious to obtain the highest productivity from those they employ.

To professional trainers these views appear short-sighted and ever less tenable as the level of skills required in the economy moves steadily upwards and the proportion of unskilled jobs goes down. The provision of support for young people for further vocational education and training in one of the ways mentioned above seems to be an area in which human resources professionals may wish to express strong views.

Compacts

First announced in 1988, the Department of Employment has established an arrangement for 'compacts' to be made available in designated inner city areas. The compacts are based on contracts made between employers, LEAs and training providers for young people, supported by their school or college, to work to reach agreed targets. Employers undertake to provide further training or jobs for those reaching their targets. In November 1989, funding was announced for the programme to be extended to all 64 Urban Programme Authority areas.

Sandwich courses　　This is an important method of introduction to employment (see Chapter 2).

Graduate employment　　The early career development of graduates has proved a thorny area for a number of reasons. As the proportion of those leaving the education system with a degree has risen, many organizations have turned to the recruitment of graduates as an increasingly important source of manpower for a wide range of positions. However, the reasons for recruiting them and the methods of integrating them into the work-force have not always been thought through.

Graduates were originally seen exclusively as management trainees, but it is widely realized now, at least by employers, that this is a false perception. Thirty years ago, there was room near the top for everyone with a degree who wished to get there; today this is arithmetically impossible. While some with degrees will naturally have the interests and develop the skills of management, others will find more satisfying careers in a specialist function, just as many without degrees will make good managers. Over-emphasis on the supposed management potential of graduates also blocks the ladder of promotion for others, with consequent loss of their hard-won experience and progressive damage to morale.

Graduates who have been identified and recruited as possessing high management potential will now normally be in a small and exclusive minority. The terms 'graduate apprenticeship' or 'management traineeship' are used to describe a structured period of training for such people. They are not, strictly, apprenticeships as the skills acquired may have little general currency and be only partly transferable.

Graduate apprenticeships aim to produce accelerated management development, using a wide range of techniques. Earlier schemes often consisted of little more than Cooks tours'—endless rounds of observation, designed to give direct knowledge of all operations within the organization—Nellie never worked so hard. Much time was wasted and graduates were left feeling detached from other personnel—destined for Great Things—to the detriment of their development and the morale of others. These dangers will probably always exist to some extent, but experience has ensured that they are recognized and limited where possible. Most schemes are now shorter and more clearly targeted, including periods of off-the-job training, planned projects and support from mentors and peer groups. Some organizations with graduate apprenticeships ensure that entry to their schemes is also open to existing employees, in order to make full use of their potential and to give a sense of fairness.

The objectives of training for graduates who have not specifically been identified for management need careful thought. Because graduates enter the organization later than other recruits, their training usually aims to make up for lost time by providing a rapid but comprehensive view of the business. Most schemes are also designed to help the process of initial job choice for those whose degree subjects have no direct vocational relevance—graduates will be syphoned off as training proceeds and they find areas that suit their interests and into which they fit.

An increasing proportion of graduates is now recruited directly into specific posts. This has become the norm for those with technical, work-relevant degrees, such as engineering. Indeed many organizations have such strong needs for these skills that they are reluctant to wait longer than necessary to benefit from them. Where graduates have studied by means of 'sandwich' courses, mixing study with practical experience, no harm may be done, but for those who have followed straight academic courses, direct recruitment may deprive them of vital experience and narrow their perspective.

Most graduates also benefit from opportunities to extend their education into relevant areas by studying part-time for professional or management qualifications, such as the Diploma in Management Studies (DMS).

Whatever form of training is given, ensuring that the graduate's expectations are realistic while also using their knowledge to the full is often a problem. An engineer with a first-class Honours degree from Oxford employed by a large and well-known company applied, some years ago, for the post of Head Cleaner as a protest about the lack of opportunities for the rapid promotion that he had come to expect. Many other organizations and their graduates have suffered in the same way—the combination of over-selling during recruitment, youthful impatience and misunderstanding of the nature of real work has soured many a career right at its start.

The Enterprise in Higher Education Initiative (EHE)

This initiative by the Department of Education and Science has the aim of helping institutions of higher education to develop more enterprising graduates. It approaches this through stimulating curriculum changes and new approaches to learning. It regards active employer involvement as essential to its success.

The EHE teaching company scheme is aimed primarily at developing the technological and managerial skills of the young graduates it employs. Companies that are planning to introduce major operational changes which will need two or more years on-the-job support can work in partnership with a member of the academic staff of a university or polytechnic and a specially recruited high-calibre graduate, for whose services a grant is available under the scheme.

Professional training

Professional training usually only begins when the individual first joins an employer and most professional institutes offer firm guidance and support throughout the early years of their members' careers. While the arrangements vary between professions, full qualification will in most cases call for a period of appropriate work experience. This may be overseen by a mentor or tutor (see Chapter 7) and possibly recorded in the form of a log. Periods of further off-the-job training may also be required—in some cases this will be provided, in others accredited by the professional institute.

The first job experience

Whatever help has been given (or not given) by way of training and education and whatever the level of the post, there is universal agreement that the actual working experience in the first job will have a critical effect on the individual's attitude to their career and its subsequent development.

It is at this moment that the chill winds of the real world strike the new worker for the first time. Leaving the ivory tower of education or training, the worker must struggle with the problems of job responsibility and its possibilities of real success or failure. Not only will systems and machinery need to be mastered, but also the far trickier problems of human relationships, whether with colleagues, bosses or customers.

These problems call for guidance and moral support, which may be made available in a number of ways. Learning to learn is a basic lesson from which the others follow. If new employees are to learn throughout their careers, they must have both the skills and the desire to do so. One of the most important ingredients in the first job experience must be the inculcation of a learning culture. This can only succeed if it is, in fact, the culture of the whole organization, at every level and for every career stage.

The manager has a key role. As described in Chapter 5, the manager can never avoid responsibility for the career development of his or her people, but this responsibility is at its peak for the new starters under the manager's control.

Colleagues, too, can have a major influence, for better or worse. Whether they help or hinder will be partly a reflection of the culture and morale of the whole organization and the quality of its management (their influence is touched on in Chapter 12).

The human resources professional has much to offer through well-designed training (this is the subject of Chapter 7). There may also be a role for specially appointed mentors—senior staff who do not have managerial responsibility for an individual but who are able and willing to devote time to meet and discuss progress and problems at intervals (see Chapter 7).

The probationary period

Probationary periods are a condition of many job offers and current legislation (the Employment Protection [Consolidation] Act 1978, as amended by the Employment Act 1980 and the Employment Act 1982) offers little protection against dismissal within two years of appointment. However, the difficulties of setting standards and monitoring, the expense of fresh recruitment and the interpersonal problems involved in any dismissal procedure combine to make termination a little used option in most organizations, most managers preferring to live with a doubtful or marginal decision—a mistake they usually live to regret.

Trainers have a clear and important role in such cases, in doing whatever is possible to help the individual overcome skill or behavioural deficiencies. It is vital that systems should exist that ensure they are brought in at the earliest possible moment. This can be achieved by an extension of the induction procedure that imposes a requirement for managers to monitor performance regularly and bring problems to the notice of the training department.

Action check-list

- Provide systematic induction training for all, whether first-time recruits or not.
- Ensure line management and supervision play a full part in induction.
- Encourage and monitor the continuing development of professional staff.
- Maintain a steady level of intakes of apprentices rather than accepting wide fluctuations.
- Recruit most graduates explicitly for non-management positions.
- Provide all new graduates with good mentor support.
- Make all possible use of YT.
- Encourage and support all young employees to undertake appropriate further education.
- Monitor and support the first job experience, with the active help of line management and supervision.

5 Mid-career development: the manager's role

Nothing can absolve managers from their key role in career development. To succeed demands moral integrity, task knowledge, effective self-management and a range of people skills.

In addition to other aspects of good management practice, trainers should help managers to accept their responsibility for helping the career development of their people and to develop the necessary skills.

Apart from the individual concerned, career development involves managers, human resource professionals and the policy makers of organizations. Each has a distinct role to play, but human resources professionals must both develop individuals directly and indirectly by developing their managers. For this indirect development to be effective, trainers will need to train and support the managers while neither usurping their role nor allowing them to abdicate. It is a delicate balance.

Ongoing management development and training should naturally cover the issues raised in this chapter, but trainers will need, in planning and carrying out this training, to always bear in mind the importance of career development and ensure that it is not subordinated to other issues. There may be a case for mounting management training events specifically to cover the needs and techniques of career development.

Why should managers develop their people?

Managers are key players in development. Without their help, the individual will find development difficult if not impossible. Managers, however, have plenty of other things to do, things that they may feel able to do more successfully and which may seem more clearly in line with their responsibility to meet production and budgetary targets. If they had spare time, development might have a place, but managers *never* have spare time—their list of priorities is too long, the pressures of the moment too demanding—so development is a job for the personnel professional. 'We're too busy for that nonsense here—that's a job for the people in personnel', is a common gut reaction.

There are many other reasons why some managers do not develop their people. They may not realize its importance, think that promotion opportunities do not exist, lack confidence, be afraid of being overtaken or quite simply because they lack the necessary skills.

For some the moral argument alone provides sufficient justification. We have responsibility for others, they would suggest, in proportion to the power we have over them. This responsibility is an inescapable ingredient of every close relationship: marriage and long-term partnership; parent–child; teacher–pupil; boss–subordinate. Of these, it may be claimed that the boss–subordinate relationship is the most demanding. A boss has the privilege and responsibility of defining, directing (or seeking to direct) something like half the subordinate's waking life—more than in any other relationship, with the exception, for a few short years, of that between parent and child. Few would seek to direct half their spouse's or partner's waking life, or the divorce rate would be even higher than it is.

However, there are practical, even selfish, reasons for managers to develop their people. Management is 'getting work done through people' and developing people helps to:

- motivate them positively
- improve their current job performance
- prepare them for more responsible work.

In the long term, the argument that development takes too much time is false. While there are many reasons why each of us works, all work best in a situation that enables us to obtain the satisfaction of growing towards our full stature as individuals. This improved motivation and the efficiency it achieves will ultimately save more time than development could *ever* take.

The development mission

Everything managers do has effects, for better or worse, on the development of those who work for them. Their only choice is whether or not their actions are controlled and targeted towards ensuring that this development is effective. Good development cannot be done by halves—as in any other worthwhile relationship, it must be worked at, it must become an automatic part of the thought process and we must develop a sense of mission.

Like all missions, the development mission will benefit from a public commitment—a mission statement. In this way managers can nail their colours to the mast and provide a starting point for action. If such a statement is made by the top person—chairman, chief executive or whatever—it will naturally have great authority and strength, but if such endorsement is not forthcoming, better a commitment by other managers and human resource development professionals than no commitment at all.

The mission statement need be neither long nor complex, but it must be direct and meaningful. It can be incorporated into documents such as staff handbooks, the documentation of appraisal schemes and annual reports; some may choose to frame it and hang it on the wall of their office. For example:

> We are fully committed, and will do everything within our power, to help every member of our staff to develop their full potential, not only within their current job, but through all opportunities within the organization.

The human resources professional is well-placed to help design and promulgate such a commitment.

Management proficiency

To develop others, managers must be at least reasonably proficient themselves. Effective personal development cannot be an add-on, unrelated to what else happens within an organization. It cannot take place within an environment of serious mismanagement, either by the organization as a whole or by individual managers. The inevitable climate of confusion, disillusion, lack of purpose and cynicism will be the worst possible soil for personal growth. No managers are perfect, but, for staff to develop, they must have few really serious failings and at least some recognizable strong points.

This is a situation in which the buck stops with each manager. As managers, each have it in their power to set things right in their own patch; they are not concerned with 'them up there', but with their own show. Time management is especially important. Many managers have problems developing others simply because they cannot control their own use of time—they never have enough for the essential personal contact.

Trainers can do much to help in this area: the better we have trained our managers in self-management, the more readily they will have the time and assurance to develop their people.

Personal relationship

'He looks straight through you', 'she doesn't even know my name'— these are among the worst criticisms that can be made of a manager.

Everyone loves to be loved from the top. The relationship with the boss is usually more significant than any other factor in job satisfaction. For most people, the periods in their career that are most fruitful are those in which their managers demonstrate that they matter to them as people. If the boss–subordinate relationship is right, the job is worth doing, whatever the problems; if that relationship is wrong, the job is hardly worth doing, whatever the opportunities.

Real knowledge of and concern for individuals is the most powerful development tool there is, without which other tools will be ineffective. To help in developing others, managers must be able and willing to enter into a real relationship with them in which they are ready to give and to receive. They must carry the conviction that they are prepared to give their people support, time, skill, knowledge, a ready ear and an occasional shoulder.

Personal involvement can go over the top. Some people prefer privacy, liking to keep private and working lives separate. They have every right to do so, if they wish, but this is probably rarer than some might suppose.

Sometimes an individual's career becomes associated with a particular boss: where he or she goes, they follow. This is often read as a form of favouritism and while this may be true, the real situation is often different. The 'chemistry' between the two may be such that they are able to contribute to each other's development in a special way. Their skills and personality may be complementary, say, or one may act as a catalyst for the other's strengths and be a support in their weaknesses.

Integrity

If a group is asked to list the main characteristics of the best and worst managers they have worked for, the list is likely to include few abstract, 'management school'-type items. Most will have a moral dimension. Common descriptions of good managers include:

- 'honest'
- 'trustworthy'
- 'open and above board'
- 'reliable'.

Common descriptions of bad managers include:

- 'untrustworthy'
- 'as slippery as an eel'
- 'he/she took the credit; I took the blame'
- 'you never knew what reaction you'd get'
- 'I was on a hiding to nothing'.

Integrity and consistency are the basis of any worthwhile relationship and the boss–subordinate relationship is no exception. Cheating subordinates can take the form of:

- taking credit for *their* achievements
- blaming their own failings on *them*
- favouritism
- withholding praise or reward that has been earned
- failing to share praise or reward fairly
- criticizing them behind their back
- blocking their opportunities for promotion
- direct lying

and many others.

Fairness between individuals in particular is essential if managers are to retain the confidence and loyalty of their people. All must feel that there is equality of treatment and opportunity in matters great and small. Justice must be done and seen to be done.

Personal example will always have an important effect. Managers whose timekeeping is bad will find maintaining the timekeeping standards of their people difficult. Managers who do not display loyalty towards their superiors will find developing loyalty in their staff a problem. If managers are known (and such things will always become known) to cheat when it comes to expense claims, their staff will also feel free to cheat.

Support

Good managers are supportive, eliciting such comments as 'He always supports me', 'she might tear you off a strip in private, but she always supported you in public'. Poor managers fail to 'back you up'. The sense of security felt by subordinates depends heavily upon support from those with power over their work and position. Managers who undermine this security will also erode their position as developers.

It is all too easy to form judgements about individuals that become self-fulfilling prophecies. Just as there is evidence that schoolchildren's performances depend to a frightening degree on the expectations of their teachers, so managers' expectations can produce corresponding levels of performance by their people. 'Giving a dog a bad name and hanging him' is not a sound method of career development.

Support is not only important for the bad times. Few things have a more positive developmental effect than creating the opportunity for people to show their strengths—not only to their manager, but to others. Managers whose weakness and lack of security demands that they must grab whatever praise is going will quickly be rumbled by their people. Managers who create opportunities for their people to shine and encourage them to do so will not only gain their loyalty but make a major contribution to their development.

Visibility

Invisible managers will be unable to help the development of their people. Managers who are too busy, too insecure or too uncaring to be available when they are needed can do nothing.

'Open door management' is a common description of the style that offers freedom to all to approach and talk with their manager at any reasonable moment. It is a combination of physical availability—the door must *actually* be open and the manager must be within—and attitude.

Open door management is not without its drawbacks. To be continuously available and approachable can cause serious problems for managers—their time management, concentration and priorities are at risk. There is also the problem of being monopolized by certain individuals to the detriment of the rest (one of the safest ways of avoiding work is to spend time in the boss' office).

Some managers compromise by being 'at home' for set hours each day or each week, others by using an 'engaged' sign or light to indicate non-availability, but the surest defence will always be the personality of managers and the nature of the long-term relationships they establish.

'Walking the job' is a highly effective method of achieving visibility and accessibility while also meeting other objectives. It is sometimes known as 'management by wandering around'. Natural relationships are almost impossible to establish from behind an office desk. Experienced managers have found that the most effective place to build relationships is the place where individuals work; where they feel relaxed, at home and in command. They will also pick up much about people simply by observing the way they work, what they have on their wall, who pops round to see them and what is lying on their desk. Being there enables the manager to become part of what is going on or to find out what is not going on at first hand and without the need for intrusive questioning and much-handled information.

Objective setting

Objective setting is one of the most powerful tools of practical development. Objectives may be long term—for example:

- to increase annual sales income over last year by at least 15 per cent in real terms
- to reduce the scrap on process Z to no more than 1 per cent by the end of December
- to ensure that the new store is open and operating satisfactorily within two years

and so on.

Short-term objectives, however, are also of great value—for example:

- to sort out customer X's complaint about last week's delivery by close of work today
- to complete the production report in good time for next week's management committee meeting.

The existence of objectives gives a sense of purpose to work and adds excitement and satisfaction, but to be more than a mere instruction, and to contribute to development, they must have the elements of a challenge; they must be attainable but stretching and carry the individual onto new ground.

If, for example, it was our job to handle complaints and customer X's problem was purely routine, to sort it out today would be unlikely to be a challenge and therefore contribute to our development. If, however, the complaint appeared unusual, customer X was particularly demanding or handling complaints was something outside our normal work, the developmental benefits of doing so could be substantial. The more such targets are set for individuals, daily, monthly and annually, the more help will be given to their development.

Management by Objectives (MBO) has been constructed into an all-embracing system of management calling for the setting of coordinated objectives at every level within an organization and for each individual. Managers review the achievements of the members of their staff against their objectives at regular intervals, updating and adjusting as necessary. As a complete system, MBO is not now often used as it has a tendency to become unwieldy and bureaucratic. However, most managers find the concept of setting objectives and monitoring performance against them sound and helpful. Such a process is currently built into most appraisal schemes (see Chapter 10).

Incidentally, there can be some confusion about the use of words in this area—'objective', 'target', 'goal', 'aim' and 'mission' are all used with approximately similar meanings. Some people use 'aim' as an all-embracing term, meaning the overall reason for the existence of a particular organization, function, project or post; others prefer the word 'mission' for this concept. With this usage, aims or missions will be supported by a number of subsidiary 'objectives'. 'Targets' and 'goals' usually describe quantified objectives.

Praise and encouragement

'Find someone doing something well and tell them so' is a motto followed by many of the best managers. However, the habit of looking for faults is pernicious and pervasive. Praise and encouragement is meat and drink to all of us; reinforcing effective behaviour with sincere praise is both sound psychology and good management. Equally, meaningless flattery and empty or exaggerated panegyrics are counter-productive.

The suggestion, occasionally made, that employees do not deserve praise for doing what is no more than their job, misses the point completely. Even the simplest job can be carried out at a range of levels of performance—from barely adequate to exemplary; praise is a natural and positive reaction to the upper end of the scale. Moreover, for some employees, attempting some jobs to attain even a *fair* level of performance may be a substantial achievement (if, for example, they are beginners or if they are striving to overcome a weakness). To withhold praise in these cases is unnatural and can only undermine development.

Delegation

Delegation is a classic development technique, besides being an excellent way of getting jobs done. For it to work, however, delegation must pass the same test as objective setting, that is, the work delegated must offer a challenge and a learning opportunity. We must define the task and the objectives clearly, offer any training and advice that is needed, stand well back, but be available to help and to monitor final results. It is critical that the necessary authority should be delegated together with the responsibility.

When manager or subordinate are unfamiliar either with each other or with the situation, delegation needs faith and courage. Yet, managers who are reluctant to delegate cannot hope, in the long run, to develop their people effectively.

Individual communication

'Communication is central to good management.' Few people would attempt to deny this statement, but there are problems with putting it into practice.

The majority of supervisors and middle managers have come up the hard way, learning to do the work they later expect from others. They thus often know more than those who work for them. For them, knowledge is power and this can quickly be modified into 'If I tell you all I know, you'll be as wise as me'. Such managers may depend for their psychological security on withholding knowledge from their people and are reluctant to divest themselves of something they feel is a source of power and protection. Others fear that open sharing of their knowledge would rapidly reveal its limitations and that to admit ignorance would weaken their position.

Such fears make effective development difficult. To develop their people, managers must be prepared to share their knowledge and skills. They are in *loco parentis* to their staff and such sharing is the most natural, sometimes the only, source of greater job knowledge. It must be freely and willingly available if development is to take place.

Communication must, in any case, be two-way: sadly, many managers are not by nature good listeners. 'Don't confuse me with the facts—my mind is made up' is devastatingly close to the real attitude of some; they prefer talking and doing and feel listening to be a passive, inferior activity. However, to develop effectively, we must learn to listen effectively. Only in this way can we acquire the essential developmental skill of helping people to solve their *own* problems; of becoming a catalyst in the learning process, rather than a taskmaster.

The skills of counselling are firmly based on skilful listening, but so also are the 'hard', task-related aspects of management. A manager who cannot listen effectively will be a bad problem solver and is certain not to pick up the clues to potential problems that sensitive listening so often offers.

Managers, like others, need to learn to listen actively. They need to acquire the skill of encouraging by non-verbal signals. They must avoid hearing what they expect to hear and concentrate on hearing what is actually said. They must hear with their *eyes* as well as their ears, learning to interpret body language and the non-verbal signals of others. This is a key area in which the trainer can have much to offer; workshops in listening skills for managers should appear far more often in development programmes than they at present do.

Group communication

Communication can be a powerful development tool when carried out in groups. A number of organizations use briefing groups—the process of regular face-to-face communication in working groups at every level of the organization—not only to communicate, but to help development. If real, up-to-the-minute information is shared and the decision making process involves all, all will grow. If my opinion is asked for and respected when given, I am encouraged to mature. If on the other hand no one asks or listen to my views, I will quickly switch off from the task in hand and, in the longer term, from the aims and processes of the organization. I do not, in such circumstances, 'belong' to it; merely give to it the minimum amount of my time in return for payment.

This is near the heart of the development philosophy. The authoritarian or paternalistic organization must, to function, 'Keep people in their place'. Policy must be made from the top down. Decisions must be made only by those empowered to do so; others must keep their views and judgement to themselves.

Such an approach, however, represses a high proportion of every individual's personality and skills and denies the organization the value they and their experience would give. Above all, it will inhibit growth and development. The organization that is committed to development will gain directly from the rich fund of their people's knowledge and judgement and indirectly from their personal growth. Policy will be made by those who must implement it and whose commitment to its success is thus assured.

As experienced communicators and facilitators, professional trainers have much to contribute in this area.

Team development

Managers need to develop not only individuals, but their whole team. Team development is an important element in the development of individuals: individual development will almost always contribute to team development—the better each member is capable of playing, the greater the potential strength of the team. To this extent, everything that has already been discussed is relevant to the development of the team. However, there must be more and occasionally the two requirements may conflict.

To develop, teams must physically meet at reasonable intervals. Purely routine meetings can be a damaging waste of time; the fact that an agenda for such a meeting can always be filled (Parkinson's Law: 'Work expands to fill the time available for its completion') means nothing. However, individuals will never meld into a team without getting to know each other and the needs of effective communication alone will call for meetings, especially if individual members work at different locations or away from base. Purely social meetings may sometimes be effective in team building, although the commonest approach is to combine business with time for relaxed and informal mixing.

The manner and extent to which managers involve themselves in the work of the team will vary according to its maturity and the changing work situation. Several approaches have been developed based on the Blake and Mouton managerial grid.[1] Professor Bill Reddin speaks of a three-dimensional model in which the task and people dimensions are supplemented by an 'effectiveness' dimension.[2] Hersey and Blanchard introduce the nature of the situation and the maturity of the team, from which the concept of 'situational management' has developed.[3]

In this, it is suggested that managers will often do best when developing a new team, to concentrate initially on tasks rather than relationships. As the team develops, the need will be for them to concentrate more on the people, while maintaining strong interest in the tasks. If progress continues, they will need to spend less effort on the tasks and their style will move into the high people/low task quadrant. Finally, with a fully mature team of experienced individuals, the most appropriate style will be in the low task/low people area (undue involvement on either dimension would be counter-productive).

Training

Some managers take the view that training should be carried out only by specialists and find this a useful excuse to avoid training their own people. There are many circumstances in which the best trainers are the managers; the job for the professional is to convince them of this and support them in doing it.

Managers will often need to train on a one-to-one basis—when newcomers join, when processes, products or equipment change, when an individual's lack of essential skill or knowledge becomes apparent—but group or team training, possibly on a regular basis, may also offer opportunities for both individual and team development.

Professional trainers should never hesitate to pass on the secrets of their craft; satisfied customers who also feel one of the club are good for trade. (Training is the main subject of Chapter 7).

Job rotation

Job rotation is the moving of jobholders to fresh jobs at the same level of responsibility and remuneration within a manager's area of responsibility. Occasionally, it may involve 'job swapping', initiated by the jobholders themselves.

It is a development technique talked about more frequently than it is used as there are problems. By definition, it may

- be impracticable in smaller areas where the number of suitable, similarly graded jobs is limited,
- fall foul of working agreements,
- be felt to be a threat by one or more of the jobholders involved.

There will inevitably be a learning curve for those rotated and hence a period of lower efficiency. However, in the right circumstances, job rotation can be an effective development tool. It is particularly helpful in remotivating employees with limited promotion opportunities—perhaps older staff—can be used to correct complementary misfits and is invaluable in broadening the experience of those with high potential.

Like all development techniques, it needs careful use in appropriate cases and plenty of monitoring and management attention during the early stages. It is not a self-worker.

Counselling

See Chapter 11.

Discipline

The issue of discipline and the role of the manager in enforcing it is not always faced. Doubts can go deep and are related to the view of discipline within the educational system and society as a whole. While believers in McGregor's Theory Y will feel that discipline has only a marginal role to play in management, other managers may feel hamstrung by formal procedures or unsure of their authority and how far it will be supported.

This is a nettle managers need to grasp in seeking to develop their people. Lack of necessary discipline not only affects task performance, it is damaging to the development both of those guilty and of their innocent colleagues. This has a parallel with the parent–child relationship—neither children nor adults can develop effectively without being clear what limits are set and knowing that transgression of those limits will be noticed and have undesirable consequences.

Many organizations fail to train their managers in the techniques of exercising discipline, sometimes even to brief them in their powers and responsibilities in this area.

Action check-list

- Help managers to commit publicly to their development mission.
- Show managers the need for balanced concern for both the task and for people.
- Train managers in time- and self-management.
- Encourage managers to accept full responsibility for the operation of their own areas.
- Train managers in the skills of objective setting.
- Train managers in communication skills, *including* listening.
- Participate in team development.
- Train managers in the full range of people management skills.
- Train managers to train.
- Ensure managers are briefed and trained in the exercising of discipline.

References
1. Blake, Robert R., and Jane S. Mouton, *The Managerial Grid* (Gulf Publishing, Houston, 1964).
2. Reddin, W.J., 'The 3–D Management Style Theory', *Training and Development Journal*, April, 1967.
3. Hersey, Paul, and Kenneth Blanchard, *Management of Organizational Behavior* (Prentice Hall, Inc., 1972).

6 Mid-career development: the role of the organization

Not only human resources policies but all major organizational policies have an effect on career development. The business plan, culture, ownership, mergers, reorganizations and long-term prosperity of the organization may have decisive effects. Organizational and job structure, remuneration, manpower planning and other personnel policies will be critical.

Knowing their likely effects, training professionals can strive to influence these both directly and in their catalytic role within the management of an organization.

The business plan and prospects

To be in the right place at the right time is the golden key to career success. Employees in a prosperous business find developing their careers easy; they are selling their services in a sellers' market. In order to satisfy the organization's needs, some may even find themselves developed further and more quickly than they would wish—they may outgrow their strength.

If the business plan suggests contraction, beneficial terms for redundancy and early retirement can help to create space and opportunity for those who remain, but the career-conscious individual will usually look outside and those with the most to offer will find openings most easily. The need to keep key employees while facing an overall reduction of the work-force presents a major challenge to any employer.

Mergers, take-overs and buy-outs

Mergers and take-overs can be fatal to individual development. The opportunities for rationalization, closures and restructuring may be beneficial to the organizations concerned and their owners, but to many employees, such measures may spell career death. In the USA, Tom Jackson and Alan Vitberg[1] speak of over 5 million jobs and half a million management positions having been lost from over 30 000 mergers in less than a decade.

Substantial and well-publicized golden handshakes given to the few mask the career disasters suffered by many. In the UK the statutory minimum redundancy payments (all that will be offered by many smaller organizations) are derisory. However, the level of compensation offered to those they make redundant in the later stages of their career by larger organizations often proves attractive. With this help, many choose to go voluntarily—either to start a second working career, to become self-employed or to enjoy other interests.

Most large organizations also now offer outplacement help to employees faced with redundancy, often using the services of specialist career-planning and outplacement consultants. The services available include counselling, job search planning, self-employment guidance, psychometric testing, c.v. preparation, letter of application preparation, help with research and interview practise. Several directories are available listing sources of this help.[2] Unfortunately, such help is expensive and may be unaffordable for smaller organizations or for less senior personnel.

Employee buy-outs may offer positive career development for those able to participate. Successful buy-outs have transformed the careers and finances of many lucky people. Buy-outs, however, require financial resources. Banks and other financial institutions have seen the major opportunities that exist in buy-outs and their interest has sometimes counted for more than the career interests of those directly involved. Not all buy-outs, sadly, are successful and even among those that are, the extra links forged between organizational and personal success may prove restricting rather than developmental for individuals' careers.

Culture and style

The culture and style of an organization will have a pervasive effect on the career development of each individual in it. Like any other society, the organization will strive to preserve its identity by encouraging conformity among its members. Those whose personal approach and skills match this style will be favoured and developed positively. Their strengths will be recognized, their weaknesses overlooked and their progress encouraged and helped. Those whose approach does not match are likely, at best, to be misunderstood. *Their* successes will have less chance of being noticed while their errors will be immediately seen. They will be in continual danger of losing promotion and development opportunities.

An organization that over-emphasizes conformity denies itself the benefits of diverse approaches, new thinking, creativity, constructive criticism and challenge. It risks becoming sterile, inbred, self-satisfied and arrogant. It may become a prey to what Professor C. Northcote Parkinson[3] has styled 'injelititis'—a freezing of the vital processes leading to mental and ultimately financial bankruptcy. Carried to extremes, there can be moral arguments against conformism. After all, it is the basis of tyranny, stifling of individuality and even freedom of ideas and actions.

Some have claimed that the day of 'organization man' has gone and that individuals now see their working life and their relationship with their employing organization as only *one* aspect of an over-arching pattern. There is evidence, however, that this is, at most, only partly true. In one study[4] James Lincoln and Arne Kalleberg describe the attitude of many workers to their organization as 'compliant flexibility'. Such an attitude, seen particularly clearly in the Japanese workers studied, results in greater commitment to the organization than to the job. Workers feeling this way will thus follow a career path that will cross skill and functional boundaries more frequently and change organization less than those strongly motivated instead towards their skill or profession.

The paternalistic culture, in which individual employee's concerns are dealt with sympathetically and supportively and that is reluctant to terminate employment unless absolutely necessary makes for comfortable careers, life-long loyalty and contentedness with the status quo. However, it can gradually stifle the drive and originality of employees and, by retaining dead wood, makes for slow development even for those who keep their ambitions burning brightly.

Also, when employers do not dismiss staff other than for the most heinous misdemeanour (such as many within the public service and education in particular) mobility is limited, making rapid development the exception rather than the norm and promotional blockages a frequent possibility.

On the other hand, if carried to extremes, a 'hire and fire' policy is equivalent to buying in skills rather than cultivating them. Individuals will be reluctant to commit their career development to an employer who devotes no effort to and allows no time for growth. Mobility will be rapid: up for the favoured few and out for the rest.

A termination policy in the middle of the range offers opportunities for a constructive career development partnership. Such a policy will not be cosy and will not cosset employees who, in whatever way, do not fit well. On the other hand, it will accept substantial responsibility for those it employs and aid their long-term career development.

Whatever policy is adopted, the practice of holding *exit interviews* for those leaving has much to recommend it. This can provide a final opportunity to contribute to the outgoing employee's development and give useful feedback to the employer on what went wrong. Such interviews should seek to:

* establish the real reasons for departure (or planned departure)
* ensure that all angles have been properly considered, both by the organization and the individual
* gain additional insights into any problems within the organization
* provide advice and support for the individual in their new situation
* do all possible to leave relationships on a basis of mutual respect.

Exit interviews may be conducted by the line manager, but it is usually more effective for someone detached from the situation to undertake them—the human resources development professional often being the best placed. The style of the interview needs to be both structured and informal, and can be demanding if the departure is taking place with some degree of bad blood. There will be a need to avoid points that could form part of any legal action and any comments must be made with the utmost care. A full and careful record of the interview is essential.

Reorganizations

Reorganizations have probably broken more careers, at least within large organizations, than any other factor, but for some employers reorganization has become a way of life. Centralization has been followed by decentralization, the establishment of cost and profit centres, matrix management, flatter management structures, intrapreneurialism and other magic cure-alls. The philosophy has similarities with the disintegration of personality in advanced neurotic illness—continual, never-ending reorganization.

Every reorganization has its human costs, which may be similar to those of mergers and take-overs discussed above. They affect not only those who lose their jobs, but those who remain, whose job content is suddenly changed, who find their knowledge and skills suddenly irrelevant, who lose friends and colleagues overnight, who are uprooted, possibly with their families (whether by a few yards or hundreds of miles), who must come to terms with new chains of communication, new responsibilities and new bosses without warning or preparation and whose promotional opportunities or departmental seniority have vanished at a stroke.

Nigel Nicholson and Michael West[5] report that more than a third of those they surveyed regarded a 'significant business reorganization or major organizational change' as the single most important life event during the previous 15 months.

David L. Schweiger and John M. Ivancevich[6] found that employees who remained with organizations after major restructuring experienced a significant increase in headaches, illness, heart attacks and symptoms of despondency, depression, anxiety and fear. They became risk-averse, protectionist, discontented and distracted from performance of their jobs.

Decentralization in particular can damage careers. The existence of a centralized personnel department has usually ensured that individuals are considered for suitable vacancies throughout an organization, but, under a policy of decentralization, organization-wide career structures may be actively resisted as symbols of the rejected 'power from the centre' approach. When the systems are dismantled, the decentralized operating units are likely to show fierce possessiveness of their best people by restricting their opportunities for promotion within their own boundaries.

These problems may, through the disorientation and demotivation they cause, limit or even offset any advantages of the reorganization, at least in the short and medium term. They should be given weight in the decision making process.

Organizational structure

Career development is most often thought of in terms of the military model—as a steady climb up an organizational pyramid. Large organizations (especially in the public sector) tend towards the rigid, stratified structures seen at their clearest within the armed forces. The clear, graded structures of armed forces, civil service, local government or the remaining nationalized industries result in an approach to careers and career development that is different from smaller and less formal organizations. The structure of any organization is the basis for the career development of those working within it, for on it job content, responsibility level, promotion, and remuneration are based.

The structure of an organization can be established by asking who, in case of overlap or conflict between individuals,

- can give instructions to whom?
- has the authority and makes the decision?
- carries the responsibility?

The answers infer a hierarchy of jobs that is the practical basis for managerial control—the 'reporting relationships' between managers and their subordinates. This control structure will be defined in the three interrelated dimensions of function, span of control and level, each of which have practical implications for career development.

Most organizations cope with the growth of their work-force by increasing functional specialization. The boundaries thus erected become ever more formidable and the difficulty of crossing them makes it harder to use the full range of an individual's knowledge, skills and interests. A production engineer, for example, who sought to meddle in the work of management accountancy would soon be put in their place, as would a salesperson who offered advice on industrial relations. Individuals can rarely cross such boundaries for promotion, except at the lowest and the highest levels; they become type-cast by function throughout the all-important middle stages of their career.

The number of levels in the control structure also affect, and may damage, career development. It is now generally considered that good management calls for the smallest practicable number of levels; for a 'flat' structure. This reduces the length of the chains of communication, makes management more flexible and responsive and allows the enriching of jobs with added authority and responsibility.

However, a flat structure reduces the number of upward steps available for promotion. In the US, Tom Jackson and Alan Vitberg[1] speak of a compression of management ranks that, in the USA, eliminated over a million jobs every year during the seventies and early eighties.

The degree of centralization or decentralization will also affect the number of promotional opportunities available and who gets them. Heavily centralized structures produce a concentration of highly graded jobs at their centre that are both organizationally and physically remote from most of the work-force.

Any organization structure can become too rigid and its maintenance and defence can become like an empire for which individual career development is sacrificed.

Jobs

Jobs are the building bricks of careers. Most careers develop through a linked succession of jobs, although a small number may develop within a single job—as in the cases of an entrepreneur whose business prospers or a professional or academic whose reputation grows. The role of the job in career development is thus fundamental and its design is critically important.

What is a job?

A job is a coherent unit of work, but there are many views of what constitutes coherency. The way the organization sees a job and the way it is seen by the jobholder are quite different. To the organization, a job is a flow of work units waiting to be handled. To the jobholder, it is a potential source of money, status, companionship, purpose, interest, satisfaction and identity. This difference of perception is the cause of many difficulties.

Jobs may be created by the individuals possessing them, by society, by circumstances, by organizations or by a combination of these. They may be permanent, temporary, part- or full-time, routine or *ad hoc*.

Job structure and content within organizations depend on a number of factors, including:

- the skills and knowledge needed
- the demands (or supposed demands) of equipment or processes
- labour practices and trade union pressures
- the patterns of training, education and qualification structures.

Each of these may affect the work content and volume, responsibility, organizational level and position, remuneration and sources of recruitment for the job.

Jobs within smaller organizations are usually differently shaped from those within larger organizations. In the smallest, there will be only limited specialization. In the small- to medium-sized, jobs will often have been shaped by the personality and interests of previous occupants or by specific but transient needs. It is always necessary to review job structure and content before attempting to fill a vacancy.

Tradition, practice and bureaucracy are very powerful factors in job design or, rather, in *resisting* design changes. It is not only that electric locomotives often carry firemen or that every plumber has a mate, a solicitor cannot plead in front of a judge and a transport manager cannot practise without a certificate of professional competence.

Specialization

'Narrow', 'inhuman', 'dead-end', 'repetitive', 'undemanding', 'over-specialized', 'lacking in interest', 'without authority' are some of the phrases frequently used to describe jobs in industry, particularly at the lower levels. It is a horrifying list and the perceptions it describes have done much to harm the image of industry. In so far as it is true, it offers little hope for effective career development.

At shop floor level, specialization has for long been tied to the constraints of the production line. Instead of 100 workers each making *complete* widgets, each individual will make some small, repetitive contribution to the ceaseless stream of *part*-completed widgets passing before them; a screw here, a dab of paint there. Such narrow specialization has long seemed both rational and inevitable—an inescapable element of the industrial revolution.

From the angle of career development it has some benefits. It enables individuals to develop a higher level of knowledge and skill than if they had a greater range of duties. For example, a pattern maker can develop finer skills than can a general carpenter and an industrial relations adviser can learn more of the case law of industrial tribunals than can a general personnel officer.

However, specialization also limits career development. The further it goes, the greater the risk that jobs may become impoverished, losing variety, responsibility and recognizable units of output. In the short term, repetitive jobs requiring limited skill will improve levels of production, but in the longer term, the limitations can damage not only the individual but the organization and society as a whole. Bored and frustrated workers and those whose skill and knowledge are only being partly used, are a major waste of a scarce and precious asset.

Today individuals are, in some cases, in more danger than ever of being penned into an area for life regardless of their potential and interests. No longer are people even computer programmers, but they are likely to be seen, for example, as Cobol programmers with experience of IBM System 40 hardware. Equally, within the professions a solicitor may no longer be a generalist, but will be seen as a specialist in, for example, cases of wrongful dismissal.

Volume of work

It is possible to forget, especially in non-manual situations, that every job must handle a given volume of work in a given time. Job design cannot be exclusively concerned with the nature and quality of what is to be done.

It is frequently suggested that modern technology will result in a reduction of the volume of work to be handled, thus leading to a shorter week, shorter days or even a shorter working life. If this proves to be the case, career development will benefit—the slave on the treadmill has no *time* to develop either as a skilled worker or a person. What Professor Charles Handy describes as the 'portfolio life', in which the individual can freely allocate time between elements of working and personal life, would, in this scenario, become a step nearer reality.

However, other pressures are at work. At national level, if the gross national product is to go on increasing, economic activity must continue to quicken; if one job is automated, the labour freed must be put to use in another. At individual level, if time and energy are left over from one occupation, many will choose to supplement their income by adding a second. Indeed, for an increasing number of people, moonlighting has already become a way of life, whether in the form of part-time decorating or writing books.

Job enrichment

Job enrichment aims to enhance job satisfaction by adding elements to a job.

The classic motivation theories of McGregor, Maslow and Hertzberg suggest guidelines for enrichment such as clear targets, visible results, responsibility, variety, the chance to grow and develop, flexibility, challenge, social interaction and skill match with the individual.

It is a trap to assume that such needs exist only for the holders of higher-level jobs; jobs may need enrichment in any function and at any level. Those on the production line and in other routine situations may be enriched by, for example, adding responsibility for the establishment and maintenance of product quality—the concept well-known under the name of Quality Circles.

Enrichment may be achieved by delegation, restructuring or by adding activities. Typically, these may include direct customer contact, the authority to negotiate or follow up slow payment or explanation of problems or delays. The lowering of functional or departmental boundaries may help, such as encouraging individuals to contribute to the costing, design or marketing of the product or service they provide. In the boardroom, directors may achieve new levels of job satisfaction by, for example, adding regular and direct customer contact to their responsibilities.

Job enrichment need not be confined to the individual. Many people find greater satisfaction from their team role than their individual job and a fruitful approach may be based on team rather than individual job definition. The design of team and group jobs has been the subject of a number of experiments, but remains a little-explored field in general practice. To many people it holds exciting possibilities. Team designs not only offer the possibility of enriched work but also the chance of career development into areas that would have been closed by the limits of conventional job descriptions.

Another exciting approach to job design is the increasing conviction that employees can, within the limits of organizational need, design their own jobs. Tom Jackson and Alan Vitberg[1] report:

Our work shows that personal career direction can be stimulated to the extent that employees can create their own job definitions, redesign and upgrade their current positions and even plunge into uncharted work territory . . .

The application of such radical thinking is likely to take a long time to work through into general, or even partial, use but matches much else that is being incorporated in up-to-date human resources practice.

Flexible hours

Flexibility, especially in regard to hours of work, can make a meaningful career easier for many people, especially those with domestic responsibilities. Part-time, flexitime or shared jobs can help both individuals and their employers. Women returning after having children can, in particular, find resuming a career easier when such arrangements exist.

Evaluation and grading

Establishing the absolute and relative value of jobs to the organization will be necessary to ensure visible justice both to jobholders and others and to satisfy the needs of industrial relations procedures.

As with job definition, there is a danger that such a process, however carried out, may focus on the minutiae and away from the main purpose of jobs, thus restricting the opportunity for growth and discouraging individual development. Any system of job grades should be a *servant* not a *master*.

Career development is made easier by fewer, wider grades, with sufficient overlap to allow individuals to develop within current jobs without the need for arbitrary 'promotion'. This is especially important if promotion would involve taking on additional responsibilities (such as supervision of others) for which individuals may have neither wish nor aptitude. The system should not force a fine craftsman into becoming a poor foreman or a brilliant engineer into becoming an inadequate manager just so that they can be given a pay rise.

Remuneration

Neither man nor woman may work for bread alone, but an adequate sufficiency of bread does wonders for motivation. Staff who believe they are paid less than comparable colleagues, inside or outside the organization, will think badly not only of their employer, but of themselves.

Performance-related pay

The pay of many private-sector white-collar workers has, for a number of years, been related to assessed performance. Merit additions to salary or profit-related bonuses are typically awarded annually. This is designed to encourage high standards of performance and to reward and encourage the loyalty and motivation of employees for whom promotion is not currently available.

Some organizations give a standard percentage increase based solely on their overall financial position. Others combine this with elements based

on departmental and individual performance. Scales based on the number of years in the post and rate-for-age scales are common for younger
employees, although a few organizations have adopted them for older
employees.

Performance-related pay schemes must overcome a number of problems
and need to be designed carefully. The mechanism for assessing performance, especially in professional and management jobs, is likely to
prove an area of difficulty. Assessors will be reluctant to face employees
with lower than average assessments, especially when they are subjectively based. Assessments are often heavily concentrated near to, but
not at, the highest level—what may be called 'the second box from the
left' syndrome. Attempts to avoid this effect by, for example, a forced
choice distribution may add to the alienation of those assessed in the
lower categories, many of whom may, in fact, be quite adequate performers.

Schemes that relate remuneration to profit or contribution suffer the
difficulty of coping with factors outside the control of the individual—
the works manager, for example, who fails to make the budgeted
contribution because of problems in the marketing area.

Performance-related pay for shop floor personnel has frequently been
resisted by trade unions. The system is rarely applied and, if it is, it
tends to be restricted to skilled workers. The move towards a single status
for all workers, however, has prompted some organizations to introduce
such a scheme.

Remuneration components
The many elements in 'remuneration' offer a range of possibilities. If the
wage or salary level is immutable, there may be the choice of revising:

- overtime payments
- shift, night-time, weekend and public holiday working
- enhancements
- performance-related production-, sales-, or profit-based bonuses or
  pay rises
- annual bonuses (for example, Christmas or birthday)
- one-off or special bonuses
- 'fringe' benefits (car, health care, pension, etc.)
- benefits in kind (free travel for railway or airline employees, interest-
  free loans from banks or building societies, etc.).

However, some of these elements can also hinder good career development and therefore need to be thought about carefully.

Overtime payments and bonuses, especially when the latter are paid as
part of a payment-by-results scheme, may hold people back: many a
skilled and successful employee has refused promotion to a supervisory
grade because the loss of the bonus would mean an overall reduction in
take-home pay.

Fringe benefits may occasionally stand in the way of development—as when a salesperson prefers to stay on the road to retain the benefit of a company car.

Pension and life insurance schemes can cause major problems for the development of those supposedly posing health risks. The engagement of older people is often virtually barred for the same reasons, an aspect of career development that deserves more attention.

Remuneration substitutes

Other items that even the tax officer cannot class as remuneration, may, in appropriate situations, be acceptable substitutes.

These include enhanced status. It is amazing, if sometimes a little sad, to see what satisfaction a new job title, especially if it includes words such as 'manager' or 'executive', can produce. The same effect can be achieved by a key to the directors' washroom, a personalized parking bay, an individual office, a carpet or a larger desk.

Holidays and time off may also be remuneration substitutes, although the length of holidays now given can, in some cases, make it almost impossible for management and professional staff to take them all *and* do the job effectively. For some academic or medical staff, time may be allowed for private consultancy. This pattern might be appropriate for other skilled workers, provided their private activities do not conflict with the work of the oragnization.

Manpower planning

At national level, manpower planning has got itself a bad name. It has managed only to produce too few teachers, a chronic shortage of electrical engineers, too many doctors and vets coming out of our ears. Non-intervention is the obvious policy for any government.

Organizational manpower planning has usually not been much more successful, but all too often, personnel policy has been reactive—careful planning can reap big dividends by throwing up potential problems while there is still time to take preventative action or make sound contingency plans. We do not need to wait for experts to construct an overall, organization-wide manpower plan; to consider the situation within our own area, be it large or small, can be an interesting and valuable exercise.

However, the problems, even for small organizations, must not be underestimated. A worthwhile manpower plan must look between one and up to about ten years ahead (a typical period is five years, 'rolled forward' annually). As with all forecasting, the further ahead it looks, the less reliable it will be.

Predictions that appear to call for dramatic action are always best treated with care. Apart from the inevitable lack of certainty, there are often in-built corrective factors that may not have been allowed for. Such a warning should, however, never be ignored—it will at least indicate an area that needs watching.

If we judge action to be necessary, the options are all likely to have implications for career development. They will include:

- enhanced internal development and training
- larger intakes of apprentices or trainees
- installation of new technology or improved working practices to give greater productivity or flexibility within the work-force
- recruitment drives, locally, nationally or targeted at schools or colleges
- higher wages, salaries or other forms of remuneration
- relocation to areas of easier labour supply.

Action check-list

- Ensure that the human resources consequences of any mergers or reorganizations are considered in advance.
- Cultivate a management style that is neither too conformist nor too paternalistic.
- Beware of the career development dangers of a decentralized promotion system.
- Limit the rigidity of functional boundaries when moving and promoting employees.
- Ensure that a flat organizational structure harms opportunities for development as little as possible.
- Take the career development consequences of job design into account at every level.
- Consider employee-designed jobs.
- Consider group job design.
- Use the widest practicable bands for job grading.
- Avoid fringe benefits that limit career development.

References

1. Jackson, Tom, and Alan Vitberg, 'Career development', *Personnel* magazine, February–April, 1987.
2. Baird, Robert B., *The corporate directory of career change and outplacement* (The Executive Grapevine, annual).
3. Parkinson, Professor C. Northcote, *Parkinson's Law, or the Pursuit of Progress* (John Murray, 1958).
4. Lincoln, James, and Arne Kalleberg, *Culture, Control and Commitment* (Cambridge University Press, 1990).
5. Nicholson, Nigel and Michael West, *Managerial Job Change: men and women in transition* (Cambridge University Press, 1990).
6. Schweiger, David, and Jim Ivancevich, 'Human Resources: the forgotten factor in mergers and acquisitions', *Personnel Administrator*, November, 1985.

7 Mid-career development: training

Career development is inseparable from *individual* development. Meaningful development should be part of a coherent organizational development strategy, almost always including training but, to be effective, a number of endemic problems have to be faced and overcome.

Professional trainers should always bear in mind the full range of techniques available to them and choose from it those that match the career development needs of the individual and the skill needs of the organization most closely.

Mid-career development is unlikely to take place without training. However, we should keep a sense of perspective—training is one tool that can help the overall process, not the process itself. The process may involve a number of other elements, such as personal/career development plans, career development workshops, coaching, secondments, outplacements, time out to 'recharge the batteries', personal study leave, special projects, action learning programmes, self-development and so on.

Development and training

The word 'training' is often used as if it were synonymous with 'development'. Training is often spoken about, especially in political pronouncements, when the context suggests that development is meant. The distinction between the two is inevitably blurred as training is a frequent, but not essential, component of development.

Training takes place at a defined time and place. It is almost always carried out by an external agency, that is, the individual is trained by another person or a process devised by others. It has defined and limited aims, the progress towards which can be measured or at least observed. It is about acquiring specific skills to carry out specific tasks.

Development occurs over a longer, often undefined, timescale. It is a series of *internal* events helped by *outside* agencies and events; people develop as a result of their experiences, which may be planned in outline, but will be random in detail. While the aims of development may be spelled out, the final results are not controllable and, as the process proceeds, it may generate changes in the aims. A batsman at cricket, for example, can be trained to hold his bat correctly and go through the motions of various strokes by a coach during a weekly session in the nets, but his development will occur from a combination of this training, his natural talent, his physical growth and his match experience. An accountant may be trained in the procedures of auditing, but her development in the profession will depend on that together with the other components of her growing experience.

Education and training

The distinction between education and training is also blurred. Education is seen as mainly knowledge-based, while training emphasizes skills. Education is generally thought of as a broader, less precisely targeted activity than training. It is likely to emphasize theory and concepts, while training is aimed at practical application. It may be vocational—aimed at earning a living—or not. In so far as education is vocational, it is sometimes described as developing for the next job or the next job but one, rather than the one in hand.

Within the vocational area, education and training often overlap in practice. Vocational education will often include elements (such as presentation techniques and effective writing) of training. Much business and industrial training will be grounded in education in the relevant theory and principles. Managers may be both educated and trained in their subject. Managers' education, if they are lucky enough to receive any, is likely to be undertaken by means of a course of between one and three years duration. Their *training*, on the other hand, often takes place through a series of events of between a few weeks and a few hours spread over a whole career.

Recent developments in vocational education and training have further blurred the distinction between the two. The emphasis now laid on competency-based training (see page 75) has produced courses, such as those aimed at National Forum for Management Education and Development (NFMED) and the National Examination Board for Supervisory Management (NEBSM) qualifications, which unite study, mentoring, structured exercises and practical experience. (The many government training initiatives and forms of mid-career education are discussed in Chapter 8).

The organizational development strategy

The field of development and training has been in ferment for several years and a number of exciting new approaches have been developed in the search for greater effectiveness.

Top up or bottom down?

It has been traditional to regard development and training as a 'bottom up' activity, initiated by the managers, seeking resources for their own staff from above. It has, like other human resources activities, also tended to be mainly reactive, responding to pressures rather than initiating action.

There is a growing body of opinion that development is most effectively carried out 'top down'. This approach begins with the definition of organizational strategy at the highest level and consideration of the business plan from which the human resources needs, including development and training, can be derived. Development of individuals will then take place according to an overarching plan within which resources can be allocated. This philosophy manifests itself in a number of related approaches, such as the concept of the 'learning organization'.

In a learning organization the total culture, from the top down, will be imbued with the conviction that to thrive and continue to thrive every individual, department and function must view their activities as a continuous stimulus to and source of learning. If experience does not offer the learning needed, it must be found elsewhere. Through the successful implementation of such a philosophy, both organization and individual will develop continuously.

Individual development programmes

Many people see the essence of career development as the matching of organizational and the individual's development needs. Whether approached top up or bottom down, plans for individual development must be created and will be crucial to effective career development.

Continuous development

The Institute of Personnel Management emphasizes the importance of the philosophy of 'continuous development', whereby each individual is encouraged and given the resources to accept responsibility for their own learning as the jobholder is seen as uniquely placed to understand their own learning needs. The approach encourages,

... individuals to develop and thus help the organisation to achieve its objectives, through the intimate association of improved learning and improved performance.[1]

In continuous development, the role of the human resources professional as a catalyst and facilitator is emphasized, as is the need for management commitment and support.

Professional development

Most professional institutions take a leading role in providing carefully structured career development programmes for their members. An example of such professional development is the Continuing Education Modular Master scheme (CEMM), developed by the Institute of Electrical Engineers, which provides modular courses with complementary syllabuses of two-week duration hosted by an institution of higher education giving an option of studying towards an MSc.

'Fast track' management development

In many organizations, by far the greatest proportion of the effort and resources devoted to career development have hitherto been concentrated on the tiny numbers of those who are judged to have top management potential.

Such 'fast track' development programmes typically begin with the identification of those to be developed through an assessment centre, an appraisal system, performance on a major management training event, during graduate recruitment or in some less systematic way. Those chosen will undergo a planned series of secondments, job rotation and off-the-job training that may last several years and which will be combined with regular and rigorous assessment.

Such schemes may be criticized as creating an exclusive élite that demotivates those not included and makes it hard for them to develop later or by different paths. They produce a heavy concentration of attention and resources onto a very limited number of individuals, to the detriment of the vastly larger numbers *not* selected. The same objections may be made at the next level down—to the frequent concentration on management development in preference to the all-embracing concept of career development. While individual development of those with high potential is clearly right, it seems unfortunate, even dangerous—to exclude the vast majority of the work-force. All can be developed, some more than others, and all should have the opportunity.

The competence-based approach

The concept of competence has, in the last few years, become central to vocational training. The Training Agency defined competence as:

The ability to perform the activities within an occupational area to levels of performance expected in employment.[2]

Professor John Burgoyne of Lancaster University defines it simply as:

The ability and willingness to perform a task.

The competence-based concept of training leads to an approach that is outcome- rather than input-based. Effectiveness is judged by changes in job performance rather than the acquisition of knowledge. This, in turn, implies training that is based, as far as practicable, on the work-place. Courses aimed to prepare students for qualifications such as those of the new NFMED (the National Forum for Management Education and Development—the Lead Body for management training) are based on a combination of short, modular workshops, reading material, self-assessment, mentoring within the work-place, special assignments and the keeping of log-books.

This approach is also intended to produce 'portable' qualifications. which can demonstrate competence in specified areas to any potential employer.

The assessment of prior learning and experience (APL and APE)

For training to form part of a planned process relevant to each individual, a method of assessment of their prior learning and experience is required. By using this, it is possible to avoid going over knowledge already learnt and skills already acquired. It also provides a rational basis for giving credit for such knowledge and skills towards whatever qualifications are sought. APL and APE are potential tools of great power in career development.

Much work is currently under way in this field and some APL centres are already being set up by colleges of further education. The approach is based on the concept of the assessment centre (see Chapter 11), although the processes are still under development.

Attendance on a programme in an APL centre will allow a comprehensive profile of each individual to be drawn up. The techniques used include briefing discussions, self-assessment, psychometric testing, counselling, gathering evidence of achievement and the assessment of the evidence to give credits against a structure of qualifications. The evidence may take the form of log-books, job descriptions, c.v.s, references and work completed such as reports, computer programmes and designs. To be acceptable, evidence will need to be endorsed by an independent person or body. The assessment process can itself be a learning experience.

APL is, by its nature, personalized and thus likely to be time-consuming and expensive. The possibility of a large element of self-assessment, possibly using computer-based questionnaires, is being explored. If shown to be practicable, it would reduce the cost of the process.

The techniques of development and training

Training is often simply divided into on- and off-the-job, but the full range of techniques is huge: in his book the *Encyclopedia of Management Development Methods*, Andrzej Huczynski[3] lists over 400.

The most common techniques and their role in career development are now discussed.

Courses

Long courses   Longer general training courses, lasting several weeks or months, have traditionally been used as a method of management development within large organizations. Based originally on the military staff college model, they aim to cover a wide range of the knowledge and skills believed to be necessary for managers at a particular level. Such courses are often linked with eligibility for promotion to specified levels and so performance on the course may be a factor in whether or not such promotion is actually given.

Typical subject areas are corporate strategy and long-range planning, financial control, customer service and marketing strategy, social and environmental issues, quality control, industrial relations, decision making and communications techniques.

The training techniques used involve a mix of lectures by senior organizational figures and distinguished outsiders, presentations by academic staff and group or syndicate work, often based on case studies. The suggestion that the most useful learning takes place in the bar after the conclusion of the day's formal sessions commands general agreement. Such courses are held residentially, either by one large organization for its own staff or by a business school or college for all suitable applicants. Converted country houses remain the commonest location.

These are the archetypes of UK management training. The combination of training and assessment has been built into the culture of a number of large organizations who are well satisfied with its effectiveness in meeting their management development needs. Such long courses have been central to career development at the higher level for many years. They may be questioned on the grounds of expense, inflexibility and status-conscious orientation and their place is probably now being eroded. They have also been used effectively as a reward—a sort of sabbatical—for loyal, long-serving and plateaued managers. Greater emphasis is now placed on shorter, more precisely targeted courses of one or two weeks duration, aimed at specific skill areas combined with separate, effective assessment procedures.

Short courses The use of short training courses, of between one and three days, is probably the commonest development activity. Such events go by many names—'course', 'seminar', 'workshop', 'conference', 'training event', perhaps 'colloquium'. The distinctions are fine and the words are not used consistently.

The subjects covered are virtually limitless. They include all aspects of supervision and management, interpersonal skills, communication, self-development, technical and specialist knowledge in every area and current concerns and interests. The range of training techniques used is wide, but the majority rely on informal presentations, group discussion and appropriate exercises.

Short courses are provided by many organizations. 'Public' courses, open to all comers, are provided by colleges and management schools and centres, professional institutions, private training organizations of all sizes and degrees of competence and by manufacturers to support their products.

'In company', or 'in house', courses are, as the name implies, run by an organization to meet the development needs of its own employees. The course may be provided by the organization's own staff or by outside training consultants.

Both public and in company courses have characteristic advantages and disadvantages. Attendance at a public course helps participants to compare practices, approaches and problems and often leads to a valuable cross-fertilization of ideas. However, the material presented must inevitably be standard and will need adapting to their individual circumstances by each participant. In-company courses can be targeted at the specific needs of those present and the practices, terminology and examples used can be chosen from the organization and its business sector. They can, if well-conducted, provide bonuses such as improved morale, motivation and team development. However, sparing so many people at the same time may be difficult and status-related or political tensions between participants may occasionally cause problems.

Short courses have a clear role in career development; they are flexible, need little time and are readily available. However, they are also subject to many of the problems that occur due to badly planned training discussed below and may consume resources out of all proportion to their demonstrable benefit.

Programmed learning

Programmed learning can be undertaken by means of texts, mechanical devices or electronic equipment. The commonest design is a programme giving knowledge in a series of sections, at the end of each of which the trainee is asked a number of closed-choice questions. Depending on the reply, the programme will branch, explaining and correcting mistakes, repeating the original input or praising and reinforcing correct answers.

Computer programmes of this type, especially when combined with video, have greatly enhanced the range and impact of what can be done and the development of the CD-ROM has further enlarged the possibilities. This device uses a compact disk to store data that can be read (but not altered) by a special disk drive attached to a personal computer. Because of its immense capacity, it is capable, with suitable programming, of providing such a wide range of options as to virtually personalize the learning process. It can also be used to offer graphic, even animated visual material.

Although exciting, programmed learning should be chosen with care. It can be a seductive toy that does not necessarily produce the desired results.

Work shadowing

Work shadowing involves observing the work of another closely over a period of time, which may vary from a day to several weeks. The trainee is not expected to play an active role in the work.

The opportunity for systematic observation of a job being done, particularly in another area, department or organization, rarely occurs in ordinary conditions. It is helpful when the work to be observed is directly relevant to, but different from, the work of the observer—a customer, for example or user of a product or service, whether internal or external. Occasionally, it may be beneficial to shadow a more senior job to which the learner might aspire. Short periods of work shadowing are sometimes included in induction training programmes, especially for newly-recruited graduates. Single days may be used as part of work familiarization for school children and can help to convey the flavour and atmosphere of a job.

Work shadowing can cause strain for the person being shadowed and that person must have the maturity and confidence to handle any potential embarrassments. The shadowed must also be willing to help and skilful at explaining what is happening and why. It can cause strain for trainees, too, who may often feel the urge to play an active part in what is happening, especially if they believe that they can contribute or that something is not being done well. Such frustrations are characteristic of those with greatest potential, and can form a serious drawback to the method.

Work shadowing is easier to set up than the use of projects or secondment, but some people have found it of limited value and feel it should be used sparingly.

On-the-job learning

On-the-job learning is, in many ways, the most natural form of training, being based on the principle of learning by doing and the natural reinforcements of real-life success and failure. The growth of the concept of competence has given on-the-job training fresh respectability.

Its drawbacks are the problems of coping with reduced productivity, failures, disturbance to other workers during training and the need for careful structuring and monitoring.

On-the-job training has, for many years, been associated with a certain lady called Nellie, although who she was and what she did now seems to have been forgotten. However, 'next-to-Nellie' is the place where on-the-job training takes place.

Nellie may well have done a superb job of training those entrusted to her care and so do many of her successors, but she has not received the recognition her efforts deserve. There can be no doubt that some Nellies can provide the most effective training available for some posts. For success, Nellies should:

- be knowledgeable about and experienced in the job
- be free from bad working habits
- be skilled, preferably natural, trainers
- have adequate time (and patience) to devote to the needs of the trainee
- be sufficiently secure not to feel threatened by a rapid and successful learner who may even surpass their own skills.

Nellies' personal skills apart, their training will, like all others, need to:

- be based on clearly defined objectives
- have measurable targets and timescales
- be supported as required by other methods, such as distance learning, manuals or check-lists, short courses, etc.

- be regularly monitored
- have the demonstrable interest and active support of their and the trainee's manager.

Nellies' efforts will do little to help unless all these can be met. If they can, they are likely to provide the most effective training available.

The Meister system

German industry has depended on a system of on-the-job training with many similarities—the Meister [master] system. Meisters are workers who have demonstrated levels of skill that entitle them to train other workers. In return for this task, meisters are accorded official authority, status and pay. It has recently been suggested by Professor Richard Rose and Günter Wignanek[4] that a similar system would be of benefit within the UK.

Attachments and secondment

Attaching or seconding learners to departments or organizations other than their own for a defined period of time is a frequently used method of development. It differs from work shadowing (see above) or the use of projects in that learners will be expected to carry out normal duties within the areas to which they are attached.

Successful attachment requires sufficient time for the secondees to acquire competence in the new area. This can imply an attachment of some length—possibly months—depending on the level of work involved. Attachment may not necessarily be continuous—just days or hours each week may be appropriate, depending on the nature of the work.

Secondment can help the secondees to learn the conditions and methods of working in a physically remote but closely related area of work to their own, such as, major customers (external or internal), overseas operations, headquarters or branches. It can be particularly useful for career development in certain situations, typically to give breadth of experience to those likely to progress into higher management or to remotivate those whose career has become stuck in low water, either due to plateauing or lack of promotional opportunities.

A succession of attachments can also be used for long-term trainees such as graduates who are expected to meld with one of the areas they work in. When this occurs, attachment may shade into induction and eventually into a permanent post.

Successful secondment should benefit both the organization to which the secondee belongs and the host organization.[5]

A special form of attachment is the senior manager who chooses to spend time performing low-level work such as serving customers, selling or van driving to combine self-development with first-hand experience of critical aspects of the organization's work.

Coaching and tutoring

The words 'coaching' and 'tutoring' are often used synonymously. However, tutoring describes help given to learners by subject experts, in the context of a specific course of study or acquisition of specific skills. In this sense it refers to off-the-job learning; being in the nets, not in the middle. Coaching can refer to on-the-job advice or to an activity that bridges on- and off-the-job learning. By definition, the tutor or coach will be an expert in the subject with an interest and skills in training.

Tutorial groups composed of students following the same course can be particularly helpful, offering as they do opportunities for exchanging views and experience, debate and general support. The ideal size is usually four to five people plus the tutor. Meetings need to be regular, but not so frequent as to demand too much time; between fortnightly and monthly is often about right.

The learner's manager may be ready and able to fill the role of tutor, but outside help is usually felt to be preferable. Few managers have time to combine regular group training with their other duties.

Mentoring

Mentoring is the making available of a more senior and experienced person to help the learner on a personal, long-term, one-to-one basis offering general, rather than subject-specialist help. It may be instead of, or additional to, tutoring. Mentoring can help in overcoming relationship problems, difficulties in studying, the application of theoretical knowledge, devising projects, offering new perspectives and insights, facing personal problems associated with work or study, self-motivation and time management.

Mentoring is frequently associated with specific training courses, but may also be of value as part of the induction process, especially when the learner has major differences of culture or background to overcome (as may happen with a newly recruited graduate). It is therefore relevant to several aspects of career development.

To be successful, mentoring requires that:

- the process be set up and monitored by a third party (usually a training expert) to ensure clarity of objectives and effectiveness for both parties
- the mentor must be interested and skilled in the development process
- there be no boss–subordinate or other formal organizational relationship between student and mentor
- meetings should be regular, supplemented if necessary to meet arising needs
- all parties must ensure total confidentiality of the discussions, unless otherwise agreed on specific points.

Mentors need not be employed by the same organization as the trainee. Provided they match the profile, they may come from the world of education, the voluntary sector or even be a spouse or partner.

Action learning

Action learning, a technique pioneered by Professor Reg Revans,[6] involves trainees undertaking a specially selected, live project within their own organization or outside. Apart from advisory support from tutors, they will join a small group (called a 'set', usually consisting of three or four) of similar trainees working on other projects. The meetings of the group will give the opportunity to express frustrations and doubts, offer and give advice and obtain mutual support.

Finding meaningful learning projects is important. Projects that do not fill a real need can lead to frustration. Finding a project of the right level of difficulty is also important. Projects that are too hard can end in discouragement and demotivation for the learner and possibly damage the organization. On the other hand, projects that are too easy will demotivate the trainees and fail to develop them. Discussions with a superior, the tutor/adviser, and 'set' colleagues can help overcome some of these difficulties.

Provided the conditions can be met, action learning can be a valuable tool of career development, leading to job, personal and organizational benefits.

The 'learning contract'

The 'learning contract' is a tripartite, written contract drawn up between an individual, the employer or manager and a tutor that specifies learning (as opposed to activity) objectives that must be met within an agreed timescale. Learners are encouraged to identify developmental needs and performance improvements that they wish to achieve. Employers will provide support, necessary resources and feedback on performance improvement. Tutors will act as facilitators and coaches, providing professional expertise and providing or finding the skills and knowledge needed for progress.

The learning contract has been used in, among other organizations, Phillips Petroleum at their Teesside Terminal. Many supervisors and managers have found that the specific nature of the obligation entered into provides positive encouragement and a clear sense of achievement.[7] See the example of a learning contract in Figure 7.1.

The problems of training

Millions of pounds and tens of thousands of working days are spent annually in enabling employees to attend courses. For there to be a return on this investment, people must have a need to go on them. Training is not a panacea, nor even the easy option it so often appears. It may contribute nothing to career development; it may even retard it. Even well-conducted training is weak when it takes the form of isolated and unrelated events imposed on an individual without plan or consultation. To work well, pre- and post-course briefings must be held, preferably as part of the personal development planning process.

Sending someone on a course is often the last resort of the guilty manager. It is the least demanding method of development—for the manager,

Parties to the contract

This contract is made between John Smith, Section Leader, Peter Jones, Manager and Michaela Green, Training Officer, all of Pink and Company.

Aim

To improve John Smith's effectiveness in the area of information handling.

Objectives

John Smith will:

- become skilled in the use of the Dataease database package
- develop an application of Dataease to one of the major areas of information handling in his section
- get the application fully operational
- train other members of his section to operate the system effectively.

Timescale

First objective to be completed by 30 June 1994
Second objective by 31 August 1994
Third objective by 30 September 1994
Fourth objective by 31 October 1994

Peter Jones undertakes

- To give whatever support and advice he can.
- To allow John such time as work permits off normal duties to work on this contract.
- To make his Dataease manual available to John.
- To give introductions to other users.
- To agree to and fund John's attendance on a two-day database workshop before the end of May.
- To check and give feedback on the results of John's work at each stage.

Michaela Green undertakes

- To give whatever support and advice she can.
- To give introductions to other advisers and users.
- To arrange for John to attend a suitable two-day database workshop before the end of May.
- To seek out any further sources of help that may be required.
- To monitor the progress of the contract and give feedback to the other parties.

Signed,   John Smith ....   Peter Jones...

Michaela Green ....   Date ....

Figure 7.1 *Example of a learning contract*

the individual to be developed and the supporting staff as it is usually easy to find a suitable course title. If presented by a reliable organization and an experienced trainer, the likelihood of generating satisfaction in the participants, their managers and their organizations is high. All concerned will then be able to feel a glow of righteousness; their development obligation has been fulfilled. However, it doesn't stop (or even start) there.

The training sequence

The logical sequence on which effective training should be based is well understood. An apparent need surfaces, either through the individual appraisal process, the requirements of new technology or reorganization or a failure to meet performance standards. The need is analysed systematically. The methods of satisfying it are considered between manager, trainee and trainer. Objectives are set, and shared with all involved. A suitable training programme or event is identified or devised to meet these objectives. On completion, achievement in both shorter and longer term is monitored against the objectives by trainee, manager and trainer.

However sound such a process appears in theory, it is rarely followed through—as all experienced trainers know. There are several problems.

The measurement of current performance

This frequently presents difficulties. While performance in simple and repetitive jobs can often be measured simply, the more complex and unrepetitive the job, the greater the problems. Performance in professional, technical and managerial work is difficult to assess either quantitatively or qualitatively.

Analysis of training needs

Even when a performance deficiency has been identified, the causes, and hence the points at which corrective training should be applied, may be difficult to isolate, especially in more complex jobs. Improvements in working practices, systems or technology may prove to be the best solution and will always need to be considered before training is devised. Picking from a 'menu' of available courses is easy and tempting but has small chance of meeting the *actual* needs. Setting precise training targets may prove difficult.

Resources

Training is costly. The direct expenses are likely to include trainer's salary or fees, facility costs, materials, equipment, travel and accommodation, but the indirect cost of working time lost by trainees must also be considered and may be even greater. There are limits to what even the best trainer and the most willing trainee can achieve with what can be afforded.

Resistance to training

Unless potential trainees accept their need for training, the chances of success of *any* training are slight.

We tend to assume that employees *want* to be trained, but this is not necessarily the case. In a study by the Institute for Post-Compulsory Education at Lancaster University,[8] Alison Fuller and Murray Saunders reported strong resistance, especially to classroom training. The resistance was at its strongest among the unskilled women surveyed who felt patronized by such training, were concerned that any upgrading of their skills might cause marital disharmony and did not relish the possibility of it leading to a supervisory position.

Many of the workers surveyed associated training and qualifications with an increase in responsibility and commitment that did not fit with their self-image and felt peer group pressure against such a change. They also realized that training did not guarantee promotion, and that there were organizational barriers that would almost certainly restrict their prospects even when trained. These depressing findings appear to have important implications that have only been partially addressed.

Trainees at any level may resist training: they may not accept that a need exists, they may feel insecure in, what to them is, an unfamiliar situation. They may fear making fools of themselves, especially in front of colleagues. They may feel insulted. About a third of the participants on a typical training course have been *told* to attend, often without knowing why or even what the course is about. It is not surprising, therefore, that many of them resent and resist what is offered.

The re-entry problem   The conclusion of a programme of off-the-job training will pose a re-entry problem that may prove the most intractable of all. The proportion of training input retained by participants after the event is often discouragingly small and the proportion actually applied on the job after the first day or two may be infinitesimal. Frequently trainees returning with the skills or attitudes they were sent to acquire find that nothing and no one has changed back at the ranch. After a brief struggle, old habits take over and all is lost.

Unless participation is part of a coherent development strategy agreed between trainee and manager, there can be little chance of its achieving measurable benefit.

Evaluation   Training in all but simple manual skills is an act of faith. While the evaluation of training has been much talked about for years, little is done. It is accepted that participants' subjective judgement, least of all immediately after the event, does not constitute true evaluation. Experienced trainers know that they are engaging in a public performance and, like other performers, know how to generate applause.

Examination or testing may, in suitable cases, check the acquisition of knowledge or skill, but the only meaningful measure of success must be improved job performance, not only in the short, but also the longer term. Unless, therefore, objectives and targets have been established before attendance and performance measured against them at suitable intervals afterwards, the effectiveness of training can only be guessed at.

Overcoming the problems   While such problems do exist and some of them are widespread, it is possible to overcome some if not all of them. The starting point must be a mutual realization, understanding and acceptance by manager and subordinate that a performance/career development need exists. This can be achieved in several ways, such as:

- via the discussion at the annual performance review and development interview
- through working out a personal and career development plan and/or learning contract
- by regular on-the-job discussions
- through the use of diagnostic instruments

As many options for meeting the need must be considered, choosing the most appropriate may not be easy, but should at least be done in the context of organization strategy, departmental goals and individual/personal objectives.

Once an option (or options) is selected, continuing commitments and support will be required, during and after the event or process. Observation of behaviour and performance after the event—fed back to the person in an honest, constructive, specific and helpful way—will do a great deal to support improved performance and nurture further growth. If we can see something, we can discuss it. If we can discuss it, we can reflect on it. If we can reflect on it, we can further improve. The absence of special measurement or evaluation devices need not deter us.[9] Willingness, time, effort and commitment—these four things change the face and effectiveness of training.

Action check-list

- Link individual development programmes to organizational strategy.
- Build a top-down, organization-wide learning culture.
- Strive for meaningful measures of pre- and post-training performance.
- Explore the possibility of improvements in working practices, systems and technology before committing to a programme of training.
- Assess and allow for likely learner attitudes as part of training design.
- Devise strategies to minimize trainee re-entry problems.
- Select from the full range of development techniques the most appropriate for each individual need.
- Resist undue concentration of development resources on high-flyers and managers at the expense of other sections of the work-force.

References

1. Wood, Sue (Editor), *Continuous Development, The Path to Improved performance* (Institute of Personnel Management, 1988).
2. *Classifying the Components of Management Competences* (Training Commission, 1988).
3. Huczyuski, Andrzej, *Encyclopedia of Management Development Methods* (Gower, 1983).
4. Rose, Professor Richard, and Günter Wignanek, *Training Without Tears* (Anglo-German Foundation, 1990).
5. *Growing Your Own Managers: The use of secondment in training and developing managers* (Training Agency, 1989).

6. Revans, Reg, *ABC of Action Learning* (Chartwell-Bratt, Bromley, 1983).
7. *Contract learning—the Phillips Petroleum Experience* (Training Agency, 1989).
8. Reported in the *Financial Times*, 3 August 1990.
9. Bramley, Peter, *Evaluating Training Effectiveness: translating theory into practice* (McGraw-Hill, 1991).

8 Mid-career development: outside help

Outside aid in career development—to both individuals and organizations—is available from several sources. Training in particular has been the subject of much government attention over many years and this is now being extended as the European Community's influence grows within the UK. Outside developmental aid is offered by institutions of education, whether further, higher, open or closed. It is an area in which every professional institution has a fundamental interest and most are very active.

Professional trainers need to be familiar with the current situation in this field. Endless changes to legislation and a succession of government initiatives have made it confusing. However, the provisions represent a cluster of resources available to help individuals in the middle stages of their career.

Government training initiatives

The UK government has involved itself continuously during the past 30 years in industrial training and development. All parties agree that the economic and social well-being of the country call for a continuing supply of suitably skilled people for the work-force and this interest has been reinforced periodically by recurring concerns about unemployment and perceived deficiencies in UK management.

Commissions and enquiries have reported; initiatives have been taken by government departments, including the Department of Trade and Industry, the Department of Employment and the Department of Education and Science; bodies have been set up and abolished and taxation adjusted. Views on the results, however, vary. While some see progress and improvement, the more cynical see the continuous growth of a well-staffed industry supported by a number of quangos engaged in the endless rearrangement of a limited number of well-worn ideas. The career development of individuals may have been helped, but the case is, at best, not proven.

The Industrial Training Boards, Manpower Services Commission, Training Agency and Training, Enterprise and Education Directorate

The first major governmental intervention was the Industrial Training Act 1964, which established a number of Industrial Training Boards (ITBs), covering most sectors of employment. The objectives of the boards were to stimulate and improve all types of industrial training within their sector. They were empowered to make a levy based on the payrolls of all organizations except the smallest in their scope and to distribute grants for approved training. The levies were substantial—the initial Engineering Industry Training Board levy was at the rate of $2\frac{1}{2}$ per cent of the industry's total payroll.

There is general agreement that the best ITBs, over the period of their existence, did much to improve industrial training within their sectors. The overall quantity of training was vastly increased and it was gradually focused on the areas of highest priority. Less was probably achieved in stimulating organizations with little interest in training to make their contribution. The smallest were exempt anyway and many others continued, despite the financial inducements, to poach skilled workers from those who did train. Partly because of the high level of the levies, the ITBs experienced continuing opposition.

The Industrial Training Act 1982 provided for the progressive abolition of the ITBs, although seven continued for a time.

The Employment and Training Act 1973 altered the arrangements and set up a central agency—the Manpower Services Commission (MSC)—with overall responsibility for improving industrial training. The MSC undertook a massive spread of work with the aim of '. . . improving the efficiency and effectiveness of industry through the development of a skilled and adaptable work-force', including:

- control of the ITBs
- Jobcentres and Professional and Executive Register (PER)
- Youth Training (YT) and its predecessors (YOPs and YTS)
- Employment Training (ET) and its predecessor (JTS)
- the Technical and Vocational Education Initiative (TVEI) (see Chapter 2)
- the Careers and Occupational Information Centre (COIC) (see Chapter 2).

The MSC has been described by Alistair Thomson and Hilary Rosenberg[1] as 'obsessively dynamic'. Under the direction of its political masters, it took over, started, changed or terminated a considerable range of initiatives. In 1985 it was replaced by the Training Agency (TA) based in the same building (Moorfoot, Sheffield) and with largely the same staff. In 1990, the operation was again re-named as the Training, Enterprise and Education Directorate, again with the same address.

'A New Training Initiative: an Agenda for Action'

In 1981 the White Paper 'A New Training Initiative: an Agenda for Action' was published embodying the then government's concerns about industrial training. It declared the need for action on several fronts to prepare young people better for work. A number of measures were proposed, designed to enhance the provision of vocational training and education, bringing them closer together, and to encourage employers to train their younger employees. The then MSC was tasked with its implementation.

'Employment for the 1990s'

The most recent changes were laid out in the White Paper of December 1988, 'Employment for the 1990s'. Its overall aim was defined as the need to:

. . . invest in the skills and knowledge of our people and build up industry's skill base through a strategy of training through life.[2]

The developments to achieve this included the National Training Task Force, the Lead Bodies and the Training and Enterprise Councils (TECs) and Local Enterprise Councils (LECs).

The National Training Task Force

This high-powered body has the role of advising government on training. It was set up in early 1989 to advise the Secretary of State for Employment and to assist him in carrying out his duties. Its specific tasks are:

- to assist with the establishment and development of the TECs
- to help stimulate the commitment of employers to training to improve the skills of the working population
- to undertake specific studies commissioned by the Department of Employment in connection with education and training.

The Lead Bodies

Some 170 Lead Bodies have been established to monitor the application of NVQs (see page 91) to individual sectors of employment. Some (such as those for Education and Training and Management and Supervision) are concerned with the needs of cross-sectoral functions.

The Training and Enterprise Councils (TECs) and Local Enterprise Companies (LECs)

In March 1989 the government launched the establishment of the TECs and parallel LECs in Scotland. They are broadly modelled on the Private Industry Councils (PICs) that have operated for a number of years in the USA.

The 82 councils are composed of top-level representatives from employers within their area, of whom two thirds must be from the private sector. They are tasked with the raising of quality and quantity of training. The form that TEC activity will take is still emerging at the time of writing and the situation is clouded by accusations of underfunding from central government and unhappiness from organizations that feel their own position may be affected. Views range from the highly enthusiastic to the deeply cynical and the only comment that can be made with certainty is that each is viewing its role independently.

Several TECs have already embarked on new initiatives with considerable potential for effective career development. Typical of those already announced are the Business Education Partnership with the local education authority to market 'careerships' and 'traineeships' based on the YT scheme (see Chapter 4) developed by the South and East Cheshire TEC. This TEC is also planning to pilot the provision of vouchers for school-leavers, enabling them to pay for training of their choice. The Tyneside TEC has formed a partnership with the Tyne and Wear Development Corporation to train long-term unemployed in the locality to fill jobs offered by organizations newly moved into the area.

The National Council for Vocational Qualifications (NCVQ)

In 1986, the government decided that, as part of the attempt to raise the national level of vocational skill, a body should be set up and tasked with establishing standards of competence for every level of every occupation. This mammoth undertaking was devolved through the TA to a body named the National Council for Vocational Qualifications. Work has proceeded from the lowest level, I, and, at the time of writing, has reached level IV—the level of the skilled worker and the lowest level with an element of supervision in a number of areas. Level V is intended to cover lower-level professional work. Doubts have been expressed as to the relevance of the approach in this area and it is generally accepted that in many cases professional competence is best measured by testing knowledge.

It is intended that agreed standards for each vocation shall be published as National Vocational Qualifications (NVQs). These will be used for the design and delivery of training, as benchmarks for individual attainment and for the accreditation of qualifications.

A lead in the practical application of NVQs has been taken in retailing by the National Retail Training Council, with Boots the Chemists being especially active. Boots is convinced that the initiative has been of great benefit and has had the affect, among others, of reducing staff turnover measurably.

A system of credit accumulation by individuals towards NVQs has been established under the National Record of Vocational Achievement (NROVA).

The work of the NCVQ should, as it is completed and implemented, help in rational career development. The structure will help people to transfer between jobs and organizations by making the validation and comparison of competence levels easier and more objective and the existence of a ladder may well stimulate individual progress.

Employment Training (ET)

This Department of Employment initiative is targeted at individuals who have been employed for more than six months, using the slogan 'Training for the workers without jobs to do the jobs without workers'.

It provides subsidized training for up to 12 months, coordinated by training agents who arrange secondment to participating employers. All long-term unemployed are eligible, but preference is given to 18- to 25-year-olds. Trainees are paid allowances in addition to their unemployment benefit and employers contribute a proportion of the costs. Those within the target group who wish to set up their own business or enter self-employment may be given a programme of Enterprise Training within the ET scheme.

The help this programme has been able to give to individuals appears limited. The Employment Committee of the House of Commons stated that 45 per cent of those referred to training agents failed to arrive and, of those who did, more failed to present themselves to employers; 70 per cent did not complete their agreed personal action plan. Of those who completed the programme as arranged, almost half were without jobs three months after finishing.[3]

It has been pointed out that, in many cases, lack of skills is not the limiting factor for those seeking employment and that for them effort would be better directed to guidance and counselling in job search techniques.

Training Access Points (TAPs)

The TAP scheme was established in 1986 and involves cooperation between the then MSC and the Department of Education and Science. It provides computer terminals at a number of locations (such as Jobcentres and public libraries) from which individuals and employers can obtain information about education and training opportunities. The database holds information on a wide range of courses.

In 1989, TAP International was introduced, developed by the then TA and the Kent County Council, with the aim of promoting British-developed education and training provision to customers overseas. International agents have been established in a number of countries, including France, Belgium, Luxemburg and the Netherlands.

Business Growth Training (BGT)

The government has been concerned for some time about the difficulties of ensuring developmental opportunities to people in smaller and medium-sized enterprises. In 1989, the TA set up the Business Growth Training programme to integrate other government programmes designed to assist smaller employers to relate training and development to business objectives and to disseminate good practice. BGT also aims to provide assistance for management and business skills training for the owners and managers of small businesses and is thus of direct relevance to the career development of individuals in this sector. Each TEC is developing its own approach to the BGT scheme.

Available grants

Career Development loans are available under a Department of Employment scheme operated by Barclays, the Clydesdale and the Cooperative Banks for those wishing to engage in vocational training of their own choice, which they finance. The loans may be between £300 and £5000.

The government pays interest during the training and for three months after its completion; from that point on the loan is on the same basis as a personal bank loan.

LEAs provide grants for full-time education. Mandatory grants are available to all whose intended courses meet the requirements, while discretionary grants may, as the name applies, be made available for others. Individual LEAs provide information on the current situation in their area.

Tax concessions

Employers are entitled to deduct from gross profits all expenditure relating to adult training, provided it can be demonstrated that the expenditure is wholly and exclusively for the purpose of the trade, profession or vocation of the employer.

Individuals must pay for education and training out of their own taxed income in virtually every case. Exceptions include expenses for attendance at external training courses that may, if not paid by an employer, be set against tax in certain stringently defined circumstances. Retraining in new work skills that employers provide for employees who are leaving or have left may also qualify for tax relief. The only widely applicable relief relevant to career development is that given on fees and subscriptions to professional bodies. (Other countries in many cases offer larger and more direct incentives.[4])

Post experience education

Post experience education is provided by the entire tertiary sector of education, including colleges of further education, institutions of higher education, business schools and distance learning providers.

Colleges of further education

The colleges of further education—the old 'Techs'—have, for many years, been a principal source of post experience education. Their role is so well established as to be taken for granted. While much of what they do is for young people, they also provide a valuable resource for mid-career education—both vocational and non-vocational.

Together with polytechnics, colleges of further education offer mature students Access courses that are designed to take mature students to A level standard in about nine months of full-time study and provide entry to higher education.

Open and distance learning

The growth of open and distance learning has more recently widened the possibilities for mid-career education immensely. 'Open learning' is the term used to describe educational courses (such as those of the Open University) that are open to all comers, irrespective of prior qualification or experience. 'Distance learning' is applied to any course in which learner and teacher are physically separated. In practice the two are often combined.

The Open University led the way in both respects. Its courses (with the exception of summer schools) no longer require attendance at a particular time and place. They are also available to anyone, irrespective of a student's prior qualifications. This approach has opened the gateway for tens of thousands in mid career to development that they could not otherwise have achieved.

The Open University has established an Open Business School that provides a number of shorter vocational courses as well as qualification programmes.

The Open College was launched in 1987 to provide vocational further education and training. Its initial development has proved difficult, but progress has been made. A number of open colleges have been established by further education colleges.

Correspondence colleges may claim, with justice, to be the forerunners of distance learning and, while the numerous private institutions vary in their aims and standards, their contribution continues to be substantial.

Books show every sign of remaining a principal source of knowledge— the most efficient and flexible kind of distance learning. More work-related titles are now produced than ever before, covering the complete range of career areas. Technology has made it easier to produce and revise books, thus providing readers with a continuous stream of up-to-date material.

Other forms of distance learning, based on the original correspondence course model, have proliferated, also benefiting from the latest technology. The Open University provides courses based on multimedia packages, including manuals, audio and visual tapes and now computer software, supported by nationally broadcast radio and TV programmes and summer schools. The Open College, traditional correspondence colleges, business schools and some professional institutions have gone down the same road. There has never been more material available.

Open and distance learning are major resources in career development. The training professional will be aware of what is available and encourage its use through advice, interest and, where possible, practical help. Organizations vary widely in the degree of support they are prepared to give to their employees. Some will provide financial subsidy and study leave for virtually any course, while others will only do so for courses of direct relevance to the individual's work and others no financial help at all. Employees whose organizations show concern and interest for their studies are far more likely to persevere and succeed than those who struggle alone and unacknowledged.

Non-vocational mid-career education

The role of education in mid-career development is not exclusively vocational. Non-vocational education can provide 'helicopter vision'— offer new perspectives, broader horizons and fresh opportunities to those in mid career.

As part of a recent wages package, Ford UK, with the help of Ray Moore of Ruskin College, Oxford, developed a scheme known as the Employee Development and Assistance Programme (ETAP), aimed at encouraging participation by employees in further education. Grants of up to £200 per employee were made available towards the cost of adult education courses of the individual's choosing. Some courses, planned by local joint management-union committees were provided in house. At least one in house course at degree level was mounted with the aid of a local Polytechnic. Both external and in house courses were taken in the employee's own time. Popular subjects included languages, computer skills, car mechanics and physical fitness. 'Introduction to study' courses were mounted at a number of plants.

The overall take-up rate had risen to 30 per cent within the first year. The advantages were considered to be improved morale and job satisfaction leading to reduced turnover. A number of other major employers are considering similar schemes.[5]

Qualifications

British Qualifications[6] lists some 1500 qualifications, of which the vast majority are directly career-oriented. It is hardly surprising that human resources professionals and managers are slow, even reluctant, to recognize some of these—especially the newcomers to the list.

Some see dangers for good career development in the emphasis and proliferation of qualifications. They feel that bureaucracy may strangle the business of personal development and that every new course may build rigidity into what should always be a dynamic and fluid area. They fear confusion and doubt over the meaning and validity of so many choices. They worry over the creation of new structures and vested interests. They doubt the relevance of much of what is taught to the small but growing entrepreneur or the manager in smaller organizations. Above all, they see those without paper qualifications, for whatever reason, being denied access to opportunities for development.

The Master of Business Administration

Pre experience business-related degrees have been discussed in Chapter 2 but the principal post experience qualification is the Master of Business Administration (MBA), which is also awarded by institutions under the aegis of the CNAA (see Useful organizations, pages 156–7).

Study for the MBA is now undertaken in a wide variety of ways. Over 50 per cent of students now study for it part-time. A rapidly growing number are studying by distance learning on Open Business School, Oxford Polytechnic and Wolsey Hall and other courses. Some study on Company MBA courses, combining on-the-job assignments at their place of work and off-the-study. A few are engaged in Consortium MBAs, such as that organized by the City University for staff of American Express, the International Stock Exchange and J. Sainsbury.

Comparatively few UK organizations are prepared to sponsor and allow leave of absence to employees wishing to take MBA courses. In the past, they have been seen by some organizations as serving only to raise the salary expectations of the holders while offering little of direct relevance to real-life management. However, this view is gradually being replaced by a belief that *good* MBA courses can offer much of value.

Credit Accumulation Transfer Scheme (CATS)

CATS was established by the CNAA in 1986 to provide additional flexible educational opportunities for students in both university and public sectors of higher education. It offers an advisory service for students on the credit rating of their qualifications and work experience and offers them the opportunity to construct a tailor-made programme of studies leading to a CNAA award. It can be of particular value to individuals moving from one part of the country to another and to those re-entering education after a gap.

The European Community

The completion of the European Community, due for 1992, seems likely to affect the area of human resources management and hence of career development more strongly than any other. It will enhance the mobility of all grades of labour, require standardization or at least mutual recognition of qualifications and the development of a range of related policies.

In 1988 a directive was passed establishing a system of mutual recognition of higher education diplomas for occupations based on courses of study at least three years in length. Work is currently in progress within the Community institutions on other measures designed to embrace qualifications based on shorter courses of study and specific to individual professions.

There is a proposal to establish a system of documentation based on a 'Vocational Training Card', which would provide a means of verifying and listing the vocational qualifications of workers throughout the Community.

Professional and other bodies

Help in career development is also available from a range of professional and other bodies.

Professional institutions

Probably the best career development help currently available is that provided by professional institutions for their members. These include the various engineering and accountancy bodies and others in professional and semi-professional fields, such as transport and distribution, personnel and human resources management, marketing and many others.

Most provide a grade structure for their members, commonly rising from Associate through Member to the senior grades of Fellow and possibly Companion. The entry requirements for each may be by examination, demonstrated experience, sponsorship or a combination of these and are carefully designed to match the progressive stages of career development.

These bodies also support and encourage the career development of their members by services such as training, conferences, journals and other publications, counselling and advice, prizes and awards, local meetings, lectures, visits, debates and other activities. Some may provide direct career development services such as job finding registers. They may have a regular journal, books and publications, short courses, library and other information facilities, career counselling and guidance.

Many will also have regular meetings of members, which can help both directly, through the papers presented or the activities or visits undertaken, and indirectly, through meeting others with similar interests and varying experience. Some see benefits for their career development in holding office within the structure.

The Engineering Council has published guidance for its member institutions on Career Management and Development Plans listing the benefits offered to individuals, employers and the institutions themselves.

The Royal Institute of British Architects (RIBA), has established Continuous Professional Development (CPD) Centres in conjunction with polytechnics or other colleges. They service the continuous updating of their members within specific areas by providing information and advice and organizing conferences and training events.

Others, such as the Institute of Electrical Engineers (IEE) have developed modular courses, in conjunction with institutions of higher education, designed to keep their members in touch with the latest developments and thinking in their specialism.

The need for those giving professional advice to be fully up to date in their knowledge has been emphasized by recent judgements of the courts. Professional indemnity insurance against such actions is increasingly sought and its conditions may include the continuous training and development of the staff covered.

Other bodies concerned with adult education and training

A large number of associations, institutions and other bodies have interests in the education, training and career development of adults in or out of employment. The selection included in Useful organizations on pages 156–7 is not exhaustive, but lists many of the best known.

Mutual improvement

Through the nineteenth century and beyond, various working-class movements arose based on the concept of self-help and mutual improvement, with the deeply held belief that education was the springboard for personal progress. They directed their efforts towards both education and training with the clear aim of helping the career development of their members.

As part of such movements, the Mechanics' Institutes and the Workers' Educational Association were founded—the later still playing an active role in adult education and training. Workers within some industries, such as the railways, formed self-help mutual improvement classes.

Community activities

For some, the path to development lies through community activities: local politics, councils and action groups; religious organizations; youth work; charities; clubs and societies of all kinds; the magistracy; first aid and police auxiliaries . . . the list is endless.

Involvement in these may contribute positively to a working career, or may produce a diversion from it (an individual will probably not know which until they have tried), but what is beyond doubt is that such activities result, for many people, in a degree of personal development and fulfilment that they would never otherwise experience.

Action check-list

- Maintain and disseminate up-to-date knowledge of government initiatives and their likely effects.
- Incorporate relevant NVQs into human resources development work.
- Support continuing vocational education for all employees.
- Consider support for non-vocational education.
- Guide employees towards appropriate professional and other sources of career development support.
- Consider and, when appropriate, recommend involvement in community activities to further career development.

References

1. Thomson, Alistair, and Hilary Rosenberg, *A User's Guide to the Manpower Services Commission* (second edition, Kogan Page, 1987).
2. *Employment for the 1990s* (HMSO, 1988).
3. *Employment Training: Third report of the Employment Committee* (HMSO, June 1990).
4. 'Tax concessions for training', DES Pickup report, (1990).
5. Reported by Martin Whitfield in the *Independent* (30 August, 1990).
6. *British Qualifications* (20th edition, Kogan Page, 1989).

9 Promotion

Promotion and external recruitment are alternatives for any but starting grade vacancies. The organization's policy and practice in this area are critical for the career development of those who work or seek to work for it. They must be seen as fair, open and flexible; responsive to individual needs and circumstances. Rigid insistence on traditional career paths, paper qualifications or seniority will make good career development harder.

Line managers' roles in promotion are vital, and professional trainers will be concerned to develop their awareness and skills in this area.

As has already been suggested, promotion is not the only and not necessarily the best form of career development and neither is it always the best way of filling a vacancy. It is worth considering briefly its advantages and drawbacks, both to the organization and the individual.

The advantages

Promotion should lead to the better matching of the growing skills and experience of the individual to the needs of the organization for the benefit of both. It should thus be the culmination of one phase of development and the start of another. It is motivational in prospect and in achievement, both for the individual being promoted and for others; it offers all a target to aim at. Promotion creates opportunities: for the individual concerned, there is the chance to move higher again; for others, a vacancy has been created to which they can aspire. As with house sales, a whole chain may have been freed.

Risks and drawbacks

Every promotion is a risk for both organization and individual. The higher the level of the job, the greater the risks for both parties. The matching of job and individual is an attempt to foretell the future in one of the most uncertain areas of all—that of human behaviour and development. Even in the simplest and most routine job, the interaction between job and jobholder will be dynamic—what is a good match on day one will have changed for better or worse by day 100.

Many careers have been ruined and many organizations damaged by a failed promotion. It may be destructive of good interpersonal relationships, especially if the individual is promoted within their own department. The promotion may be too rapid, stretching the individual too far, endorsing the famous 'Peter Principle', which claims that individuals are likely to be promoted to 'their level of incompetence'.

The effects of promotion are not limited to the individual chosen but will extend to many others. Individuals who are not given the promotion they believe (rightly or wrongly) they deserve may become disillusioned and demotivated. Depending on circumstances, they will either perform less well in their current job or move away, possibly outside the organization.

For the individual, it takes considerable strength of character to turn down an offer of promotion, but to accept an unsuitable offer may do immense, possibly irreparable harm to a career. The dangers include:

- accepting a job for which the individual is not well fitted, which stresses too much or challenges too little
- moving into a team with whose members they do not meld or an organization whose culture is alien
- relocating the family in a way or to a place that creates personal stress, educational problems or disrupts the spouses' or children's working or social life.

Promotion policy

This formidable list of potential problems underlines the importance of sound promotion policies. Promotion and career development are not synonymous, but mistakes in promotion can ruin years of developmental effort.

Promotion is first, of course, an act of selection. The selection mechanism must be appropriate and effective. This has been discussed in Chapter 3. However, promotion is concerned with taking on more responsibility and challenging work. It requires a person, usually, to be more self-reliant and competent and with different 'support mechanisms'. This can be considered pictorially as shown in Figure 9.1.

Promotion usually involves matching individuals to an existing job vacancy. More rarely, a job may be created to match an individual who is seen as possessing particularly valuable skills, great potential or who has just received an irresistible offer from a rival organization. Unless part of a long-term development strategy, such moves are rarely successful for either employer or employee—panic reactions should be resisted.

Visible justice

Promotion is an area in which justice must be both done and seen to be done. Employees prefer a process that is open, professional and gives confidence that choices are well and honestly made.

The process itself should be generally known and always followed. If the mechanism is secret or varied according to the whims of managers, however senior, it will create no confidence. Full internal advertising of vacancies helps to create a climate of fairness and openness and can

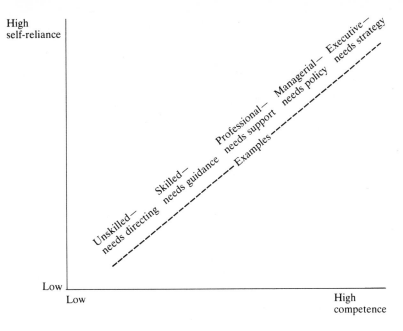

Figure 9.1 *Promotion as a function of reliance and competence*

limit various forms of discrimination. The Equal Opportunities Commission has for this reason made clear[1] that it believes that internal vacancies should be advertised

Promotion by nomination is widely practised in smaller organizations in which formal and complex procedures are inappropriate, but this method can be demotivating without the safeguard of open discussion with all who are affected.

'Make or buy'

The most important single policy aspect is whether the organization habitually looks inside or out when filling vacancies above the starting grade. Theoretically, the decision should depend on the circumstances of each case; in practice, organizations tend to look first in one direction or the other.

Organizations that look first outside believe that the requisite skills are unlikely to be found among their existing employees, that an injection of 'new blood' is beneficial or that promotion from within may cause interpersonal tensions among colleagues.

Organizations that look first inside believe that it is important for employees to have the opportunity to develop with the organization and to know that they have this opportunity. They will feel that the knowledge of the organization of its existing employees is an important asset. They believe that, because organization and individual are already well known to each other, the danger of a misfit in the new post will be less. The direct cost of internal recruitment will certainly be less than of recruitment from outside.

Most organizations accept that the case for internal recruitment is the stronger, but, the more senior the post, the more likely they will be to look outside. The problem can be most acute when filling board-level positions or the top job itself. However, the demotivating effects on senior employees can be seriously damaging—so much so that they will start to look outside for promotion and thus give further credence to a self-fulfilling prophecy benefiting no one but head-hunters.

Promotion by seniority

Promotion by seniority is common for hourly paid or wages grade employees or the junior clerical posts of larger organizations. The policy of promoting the senior suitable applicant within the grade may be embodied in an agreement between employer and trade union.

Such a policy is felt to be fairer, reducing the risk of favouritism and discrimination. It gives a sense of security to individuals, who can often calculate the likely date of their next promotion months or years ahead. It can be claimed that the chances of a good choice are as high as with the all-too-often badly conducted processes of selection. It certainly reduces the administrative load and burden of responsibility for promotion.

Promotion by seniority makes active career development harder. There are risks of unsuitable individuals being promoted and of the loss of management control. In most cases, seniority will mean age and so younger employees, ripe for development, may find that the way forward is blocked, possibly until their will to progress has been blunted. If, however, the most senior applicant is *not* promoted, bitterness is likely to be felt both by those passed over and their colleagues and industrial relations procedures may be invoked. Occasionally there may be difficulty in establishing whether an individual falls within the appropriate grade.

Ladders and paths

'Ladders of promotion'—the sequence of posts of rising seniority through which employees from a given starting grade pass as they are promoted—are based on function and level but may be even more specific. A classic example for over a century was that of the railway engine cleaner who would, in course of time, be promoted to fireman, 'passed' firemen would then be allowed to drive, then become qualified drivers in the lowest 'link' (or group of duties) and so on until they reached the top link, responsible for the most important passenger trains.

Such ladders may be based on organizational structure, qualifications, professional hierarchy or tradition. They may be enshrined in agreements or practice—even law. It would be impossible, for example, to appoint a judge who had not practised as a barrister. They are a guiding light for career development and a useful rule-of-thumb for recruitment and promotion.

The 'career path' to date of any candidate for promotion is one of the first aspects the candidate is judged on. Those who have deviated from the established norm are viewed askance, the more so the greater the deviation.

Often there may be valid reasons for insisting on a specific career path; without it, for example, applicants may lack essential experience. However, career paths make better servants than masters, both for manager and employee. The human resources function cannot escape blame. Indeed, many of the classic preconceptions as to what constitutes a 'good c.v.' originate from this area, in which almost anything that is unusual—that deviates from a standard career path—is a cause of doubt. Even aspects of the c.v. such as a period of self-employment are viewed askance by some employers and the reasons for wishing to leave and then re-enter paid employment are thought to be deeply suspicious. The preliminary sift of job applications before interview, often completed by personnel staff alone before discussion with the managers involved, probably has a baleful effect on the career development of many people.

Such judgements may be too simplistic, so that lack of certain experience may not matter as much as we think or may be counter-balanced by other advantages. To judge candidates for recruitment or promotion too rigidly by their career paths may be a form of unacknowledged discrimination—a subconscious 'not one of the club' syndrome. To promote and train someone with good potential but an unusual career path may not only provide excellent career development for them, but also be more effective than picking an inferior candidate with a conventional career path.

Parallel promotion ladders

Some organizations provide 'parallel promotion ladders'. These enable individuals to move upwards either by accepting management responsibility or equivalently graded technical posts. Thus, an engineer may have the option of promotion to the position of either engineering manager or of senior engineer, both carrying the same salary and status (an example is given in Figure 9.2). Without this option, a fine engineer (or whatever) may be forced into the role of a poor, unwilling manager. In its absence, for example, many inspired classroom teachers have been promoted to headteachers for which they have neither the interest nor the expertise—the system loses a fine teacher and gains a poor manager.

Not every sector or every organization has yet applied this lesson. The career development of many technical experts still depends on their acceptance of management responsibility, despite general agreement that management is a skill in its own right.

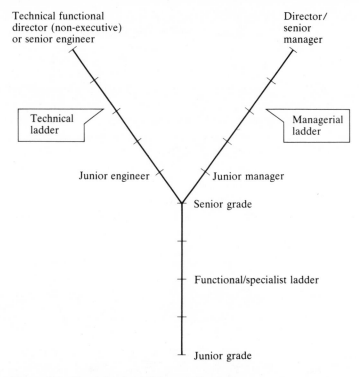

Technical functional
director (non-executive)
or senior engineer

Director/
senior
manager

Technical
ladder

Managerial
ladder

Junior engineer

Junior manager

Senior grade

Functional/specialist ladder

Junior grade

Figure 9.2 *Example of parallel promotion ladder*

Promotion bars

Many organizations impose bars at certain stages on the promotion ladder, either explicitly or by custom and practice. The clearest case of this is the barrier between 'other rank' and commissioned officer status in the armed forces.

Similar discontinuities exist in civilian promotional ladders—some clearly copied from the forces model. The commonest is the 'blue/white collar' split—the split between hourly paid and salaried employees. Some large organizations may further subdivide into weekly, fortnightly or monthly staff, or director, executive and other management levels.

In the senior professions—medicine, accountancy and the law—the principal barrier is between professionally qualified and unqualified employees. A similar arrangement exists in some other professions, such as banking, and has been established in recent years within engineering.

While few organizations outside the armed forces provide employees with indications of rank to be worn on the sleeve, the distinctions are clearly shown in other ways. Substantive differences of payment methods, pension arrangements and promotional procedures are supplemented by an array of other status indicators, such as entitlement to a carpet or a larger desk, eating and car parking arrangements. Status and its symbols can become a serious factor in career development—job titles, reporting relationships, reserved parking spots or a key to the executive washroom may be acceptable in place of promotion. This has provided an answer to the problem of many a plateaued manager.

The restrictions such promotional bars create for career development can be unsurmountable and the proliferation of qualifications in recent years has increased their number and strength. The distinction, for example, between graduate status engineers and non-graduate engineering technicians is regretted by those who saw the possibility of development from craft apprentice to fully-qualified engineer as beneficial to the individual and to the organization and productive of some of the finest engineers.

Outside the professional field, an increasing number of organizations within the UK, led by Japanese-owned companies, have opted for single status and common conditions for all employees.

Job succession planning

Responsible managers will always be considering who should replace them, either temporarily or permanently, and the responsible organization will then have succession plans for its key jobs.

Within large organizations, succession plans can reach the complexity of a spider's web and may take on a life of their own, but the panic and problems that sudden death or departure from a senior post can cause is enough to convince those who have experienced it of the need for contingency planning. As with other aspects of career development, the need is for responsiveness and flexibility. Plans that are too rigid strangle development; it is no answer to the question 'Why did she not get the job?' to say only 'Her name was not on the succession plan'.

A simple test of whether the plan is too simple or too complex is to ask the question about key post holders, 'What would happen to the company if they were run over by a bus?' If the answer is 'nothing', and several people are being groomed for it or the answer is 'We'd be in a mess' and no one is available to take over, succession planning is not working effectively. Another way is to examine the key accountabilities of the job, how they relate to organizational success and what staff are available with the competence and reliability to handle them. A management/staff audit may well be necessary in order to answer such questions.

The evaluation of c.v.s or, résumés

There are a number of arbitrary criteria often used by human resources staff and managers for judging whether a career has been well-developed. These include:

- an obvious connection between successive posts held
- only acceptable reasons for job changes ('acceptable' including 'greater scope/responsibility', etc:, 'unacceptable' including 'failure to get on with boss/colleagues', 'wrong job choice', 'dismissal/enforced redundancy/asked to leave', etc.)

- job changes neither too frequent nor too far apart, bearing in mind the stage of career reached (see below)
- a steady salary/wages progression—the steeper the climb, the better the development is felt to be
- few changes of employer and all changes fully and acceptably explained ('acceptable' and 'unacceptable' being defined in much the same way as job changes, although acceptable reasons may also include bankruptcy, take-over and major reorganization)
- no gaps in employment, unless fully and acceptably explained (in this case 'acceptable' tends to be more stringent).

In fact, such arbitrary criteria may often be superficial and unimportant. They may suggest prima-facie evidence that further examination shows to be misleading. There are no short cuts to the sound evaluation of an individual's career development.

The period between promotions

The ideal career would consist of a series of perfect matches between individual and job, but, unless the job also develops along with its holder, the match will become less and less perfect and the need for a job change become progressively more pressing.

It is common for selectors to judge the c.v. of a candidate for promotion in terms such as 'He wasn't in that job long', 'The dust doesn't seem to have settled on her feet' or 'He seems to have got stuck there for an awfully long time'. Such reactions are based on an arbitrary model of career development that job tenure should not normally be less than two years in the early stages of a career, stretching to three or four by mid career, and that anything over five years would, until after the age of 40, be condemned as too long. One danger of this model is that speed of promotion may be judged as competence, thus becoming a self-fulfilling prophecy. As in so many aspects of career development, generalizations are dangerous.

Most large organizations have a mechanism for identifying those they believe to be 'high-flyers' or who should be placed on the 'fast track' for accelerated development, but this may not be a helpful approach, as discussed in Chapter 11.

The manager's role

Promotion can be a severe test of managers' wills to develop their staff. There are several difficulties.

If the promotion is to a post outside their area, it will deprive them of an effective member of staff. It will demonstrate whether they are prepared to help others to reach, or even surpass, their own level. It may demand acceptance that an individual is threatening their own position or leapfrogging over them. It will certainly create the need to face consequent staff moves and the associated difficulties. It will show whether they are more concerned for a job to be done well or for the person who does it well. Managers must not block promotion for their people, for, even if they believe this to be justified, they would be hard put to avoid the appearance of jealousy and uncaring obstruction. The temptation to hold back good people can be strong, but it is always evil.

Good managers will keep in touch with changes within the organization that might provide openings for their people and will value tips and general support in doing so from the human resources professional, who may often have a wider view and more contacts.

If opportunities for advancement do not exist in their own organization, they may be presented with the challenge of guiding and even helping good people to develop elsewhere. While this will always need careful thought, to do so will not only be a moral duty but an added motivation to the individual concerned and to their colleagues.

Managers must always be ready for frank discussion of the promotion situation and any problems—organizational or individual—that exist. This is a natural part of the process of appraisal (see Chapter 10), but, further, they must be prepared to talk about promotion whenever it is on someone's mind. They must be as sensitive to opportunities as their people. Few things give employees greater confidence than the feeling that their superior is genuinely keen to help them upward.

The way in which promotion is actually offered can help or hinder. Sometimes, especially if there has been no formal selection process, the act can resemble the laying on of hands rather more than a critical stage of career development—'Well, Bill, you're Project Manager, now—off you go, and the best of luck!'

Even if there is reason to believe that the people have already gained good knowledge of the job to be done, managers must take the utmost care to brief them, not only in the formal list of duties and responsibilities, but in the special contribution expected of them. It is most unlikely that such a briefing could ever be completed in one session; in most cases, a process of systematic induction will be essential (see Chapter 4).

In summary, promotion and career development are both very much part of the road to success for both individual and organization. However, the route needs careful mapping.

Action check-list

- Help all concerned to understand the true role of promotion and promotion policy in career development.
- Encourage managers and human resources professionals to adopt a flexible approach to career paths, qualifications and seniority.
- Challenge the validity of any promotion bars within the organization.
- Help managers to develop the approach and skills necessary for their role in the promotion of their people

- Ensure promotion procedures are fair and seen to be fair
- Encourage full consideration of the claims of internal candidate
- Provide parallel technical and managerial promotion ladders.

Reference

1. *EOC Code of Practice* (HMSO, 1985).

10 Mid-career evaluation: performance appraisal

Regular, systematic performance appraisal of individuals is near the core of career development. However, appraisal is not universally popular and so to succeed a scheme must be carefully devised and skilfully applied. Some schemes also help individuals to draw up and review their personal career development plans. Appraisal should look to the past, considering the extent to which objectives have been met and the reasons for any failures. It should also look to the future, setting new objectives, deciding whether changes in methods or technology are needed, and what managerial or developmental support is necessary, and identifying training needs. Not only the appraisee, but the manager, colleagues and other parts of the organization should benefit from this review.

For success, appraisal calls for direct intervention by the training professional, often in helping to devise an effective scheme and always in ensuring that appraisers and the others involved are fully trained.

Appraisal is the Joker of career development. In theory, it should be of central value, but in practice it can even be counter-productive. While some believe the problems associated with the process can be avoided by good design and professional application, others are convinced that they are endemic. It is worth examining both angles. To have a chance, the appraisal must have top management support and be systematic, as the effectiveness of such schemes is undoubtedly sensitive to the methods used, the skills of those involved and the thoroughness of the follow-up. It must be regular (not less than once a year) to ensure that changes in the job, the individual and the environment are taken into account. Such regular appraisal is distinct from the rarer, *ad hoc* reviews that help in long-term career planning (these are discussed in the next chapter).

The benefits of appraisal

Appraisal can help individuals, their colleagues, managers and the whole organization. It should look both to past and future.

The appraisal gives an opportunity to review past successes and failures and identify and agree the causes of them. These may be:

- personal (such as lack of skill, knowledge or motivation)
- external (such as lack of material, equipment or other resources)

- the result of inadequate supervision or failures of systems or organization
- interpersonal difficulties with colleagues, customers or others.

In looking to the future, appraisal can help towards long-term problem solving. It should contribute to:

- effective communication
- team building
- the consolidation of good boss–subordinate understanding.

It is the ideal opportunity to:

- set short-, medium- and long-term objectives and gain commitment to them
- identify any need for additional resources, development and training
- consider career problems, establish any need for long-term review and, if necessary, major changes of direction
- make or review a personal career development plan.

An appraisal is not the time to administer reprimands or make criticisms that have not already been made in the normal process of management. It is the occasion for these to be reviewed, put into perspective and related to the future.

The problems of appraisal

Appraisal is a process that can raise doubts or, sometimes, direct opposition. Most larger organizations operate appraisal schemes for at least some of their employees, although the purpose and methods vary widely, but their effectiveness is in the hands of administrators and managers who may have reservations about their value. When done half-heartedly, appraisal can do more harm than good. There are also those who challenge the basic concept—witness the long-running conflict in education.

Problems often stem from lack of clarity about the purpose of appraisal and possible aims may be mutually contradictory. Appraisal may be seen by some as primarily evaluative—for them the aim is to judge how well employees have performed and to let them know. Others regard evaluation as anathema—for them the aim of appraisal is to strengthen communication between colleagues, to help team building, to engage in joint problem solving and to help individuals produce career development plans. Some appraisal schemes are designed to be the basis for financial reward so may include point scoring and mathematical formulae to arrive at the appropriate level of bonus or salary. Other schemes distance themselves as far as possible from anything to do with payment.

The process of appraisal is very time-consuming and the onset of the annual round is frequently contemplated with horror by hard-pressed managers and human resources professionals. A common feeling is that, irrespective of other doubts, the process is not cost effective.

At the personal level, some managers and jobholders regard appraisal with deep suspicion. It may be felt that appraisal:

- may provide opportunities for appraisers to exercise personal bias and bad feeling, political influence or transient fashions of thinking
- can upset those who cannot take criticism
- is unduly time-consuming
- demands too high a level of interpersonal skill from the appraiser
- cannot do anything to help long-serving employees
- can pose problems in the way it affects bonus or salary
- is made ridiculous if agreed actions are not followed up effectively
- depends on procedures, discussions and documentation that are not leakproof.

The interview is the cause of greatest stress for both appraisee or appraiser. Appraiser's anxieties can include:

- facing individuals with less than excellent performance
- becoming involved in controversy or highly personal situations
- over-emotional reactions from the interviewee
- being drawn into making promises they will have difficulty in honouring in regard to promotion, pay, training or transfer
- facing those whose careers have plateaued and for whom there is no apparent way forward.

Appraisees worry about:

- the judgements that may be passed on them and how fair they may be
- the need to fight their corner with their manager over doubtful or difficult issues
- the best way to register any disagreement they may feel is necessary.

Appraisal can be the subject of organized opposition by trade unions and other employee organizations. Indeed, there has been bitter and long-term resistance to appraisal in some areas, such as school teacher appraisal. While it has been widely implemented in professional and management grades within the private sector, manual employees are rarely covered. When such grades are covered, schemes usually lay more emphasis on the link with remuneration and less on career development.

The history of appraisal systems

In an attempt to maximize the benefits of appraisal, both the aims and methods of appraisal schemes have changed in recent years. When first introduced, they were frequently secret. In some schemes the report—even the existence of the process itself—was not revealed to the appraisee. Some employers revealed part of the appraisal to the employee while keeping the remainder, which often included comments by a senior manager and an assessment of promotion potential, secret.

Appraisal frequently took the form of an annual report on the employee. Some, typically in public services, were free-form written reports. Others were based on the subjective scoring or rating of traits, performance and potential on a series of scales. Some combined both approaches.

The amount of paperwork in earlier schemes was often substantial and included proformae to be completed by the appraisee, appraiser, the appraiser's manager and the personnel department.

Schemes have become more open, with most now being entirely open to the appraisee. The assessment of personality traits has been replaced in many schemes by the most objective measures of performance that can be established, often against pre-set targets. Rating scales have, in many cases, been replaced with written descriptions. Some schemes now rely heavily on self-assessment by the appraisee. The volume of paperwork has in most schemes been substantially reduced.

Personal development planning (PDP)

Some schemes now provide for the making and subsequent review of personal career development plans as part of the process. This allows a clearer separation between the backward- and forward-looking elements. The backward look—the performance appraisal proper—can then be more explicitly linked to remuneration and may be completed as part of what is, theoretically at any rate, a separate process. The forward look—the personal development plan—can be detached from this and concentrate on matching the individual's aspirations and skills with the needs of the employer and providing appropriate development and training.

Successful appraisal schemes

If an appraisal scheme is to have a chance of success, some of the following are essential ingredients:

- clear, agreed aims
- visible management commitment from the highest level
- simple, well-designed paperwork
- planned and careful introduction of the scheme
- thorough training of all involved
- effective interviewing
- the recognition of potential
- systematic follow-up.

Each of these is now discussed.

Clear, agreed aims

The first question to be resolved must be 'Why appraise at all?' What benefits are hoped for from the introduction of a scheme? The potential benefits will need to be applied to the specific situation and needs of each organization. A series of questions about existing systems will help, such as how:

- are short-, medium- and long-term objectives now set?
- are development and training needs now established?
- are organizational problems now identified?
- are individuals helped to produce and review career development plans?
- is performance now measured and fed back?
- do managers receive feedback on their own performance?
- are the available skills, experience and interests matched to the overall needs of the organization?
- is potential now assessed?
- is reward now controlled?

To be justified, an appraisal scheme will have to offer clear improvements in some or all of these areas.

An appraisal scheme cannot be grafted on to a completely different management style. An open, two-way approach would not work in a closely structured and hierarchical organization and a tight, evaluative scheme would be wrong for an informal, loosely structured company. Participative managers who try to be authoritarian in appraising their subordinates, or vice versa, will be unconvincing and ineffective.

Career development is helped by non-evaluative appraisal schemes separated as clearly as possible from decisions about remuneration. This approach encourages positive, two-way discussion and feedback and an atmosphere in which longer-term career aspirations can be fruitfully explored (this approach is followed in the PDP schemes mentioned above). Highly evaluative schemes will produce a defensive, backward-looking and often negative approach in both parties that will do little to address the major career issues.

Visible management commitment

A successful appraisal scheme depends (as the author once found himself pointing out to a group of churchmen, including two bishops) on visible commitment from the highest level. It is ideal if all employees can be covered and be *shown* to be covered by the same scheme. Chief executives who can tell their people that they are subject to the same appraisal process as them have better chances of carrying conviction and the same is true for every step on the management ladder. The boss who says 'this rather unpleasant experience is good for you but not for me' is on a hiding to nothing.

Simple, well-designed procedures and paperwork

It is most common to appraise each individual annually, although special schemes for fast track trainees may call for six- or even three-monthly appraisal. A few schemes reduce the frequency of appraisal for employees in the later stages of their career. Many schemes conduct all appraisals according to a standard timetable, some calling for them to be carried out on the anniversary of the individual's appointment. The latter approach creates an atmosphere of concern and avoids peaking of work for appraisers, but it can only be used if appraisal is divorced from decisions about remuneration.

Systematic appraisal requires effective administration, which is usually provided from within the human resources area. This will include initiation of each round of appraisal, supply and control of documentation and the progressing of all concerned (often the hardest task). While appraisal should *not* be a bureaucratic process, it can all too easily become one (many schemes have sunk under too much paper).

The heart of successful appraisal is discussion, but the results of the discussions—especially such items as objectives or standards agreed, development needs that have been identified and the follow-up necessary—will need to be accurately recorded. These records may also need to be communicated to others in order that appropriate action can be taken.

The best paperwork format will depend on the design of the scheme, which in turn must depend on its exact purpose and the management style and culture of the organization. A few schemes rely on blank sheets of paper on which a free-form record of action points can be recorded. While the blank sheet of paper is attractive, it is likely that a skeleton proforma or check-list of areas to be covered is the practical minimum (an example is given in Figure 10.1 at the end of this chapter).

Whatever paperwork is used, adequate arrangements must be devised to keep it confidential at every stage.

Planned and careful introduction of the scheme

Much of a scheme's chances of success will depend on the way it is first introduced.

Genuine consultation with all at an early stage, inviting comments on and inputs to what is being planned, is essential. The collective wisdom of everyone concerned is likely to improve the scheme and the opportunity to contribute will strengthen commitment.

When the details have been finalized, they will need to be written up, possibly in several formats: there must be a full description—a bible—answering all questions. There will also need to be a shorter, simpler guide for general distribution to both appraisers *and* appraisees (separate guides for each generate suspicion and if the scheme is generally applied, many people would, in any case, need both). Written briefing on the purpose and procedures of the scheme will always need to be supplemented by face-to-face discussion between individual appraisers and appraisees.

When new individuals are brought within the scope of the scheme through recruitment, promotion or transfer they will also need written and face-to-face briefing. This should become an element in the induction process.

Appraisal schemes should be reviewed at reasonable intervals (every five years is about right) or whenever major changes in the ownership, strategy or operation of the organization occur. Such reviews will only be valid if they involve top management.

Thorough training of all involved

The training of appraisers is essential. In the long run, more schemes fail through unskilled appraising than for any other reason. Unskilled appraisers will be reluctant to undertake the process and, if they do carry it out, they will appraise less effectively and be more likely to cause misunderstandings and upset their appraisees.

Training in the skills of interviewing is essential. The processes of actually making the necessary judgements and of completing paperwork is an aspect that is sometimes neglected during training, but should be included in any programme. Exercises aimed to improve the consistency and reliability of appraisal judgements must be tailor-made for individual schemes but are fairly straightforward to devise. If the scheme emphasizes career development planning, this will call for additional elements in the training of appraisers. The training should be topped up by a short, perhaps half-day, session as part of the introductory procedures to each fresh round. Appraiser training is most frequently based on role-played interviews that can be videoed and played back to provide feedback to the participants.

Training of appraisees is less common, but can be of great value. Interviewees who are too nervous, too defensive or fail to understand the objectives and procedures of the scheme will benefit less and confer less benefit on their manager and organization.

Effective interviewing

The interview is central to the success or failure of appraisal. Guidelines for successful appraisal interviewing include:

- careful preparation
- clear interview objectives
- an appropriate choice of style
- good introductory phase
- effective use of questions
- active listening and interpretation of body language
- confrontation of problems
- clear target setting
- a good conclusion.

The importance of training in achieving these can hardly be over-emphasized.

The recognition of potential

The identification of potential is part of the forward look of every appraisal and essential to its value in career development. However, if the military model of career development—the climb up the pyramid—is followed, this can be a cause of difficulty. If appraiser or appraisee see career development *only* in terms of promotion this aspect of appraisal is likely to be either hypocritical or disappointing. Appraisers will then often feel under pressure either to say something that they know is not true or to wreck what has been achieved by denying that the appraisee has promotion potential. Managers may also feel the urge to record promotion potential for individuals who have served them well or even those they have had to criticize as a sort of quid pro quo.

If discussion of potential is not mandatory, the problem will be minimized, but this drains appraisal of one of its most valuable contributions to career development. As was said earlier, the approach to appraisal must be consistent with the style and culture of the organization. If this incorporates the military concept of career-by-promotion, there can be no escape at this point; those without promotion potential must be told so. Whatever philosophy is held, though, the discussion of potential should broaden into the individual's life objectives inside and outside their present job and the production of a viable career development plan. The point at issue should not be 'What promotion can the organization offer you?' but 'What are your personal objectives for the foreseeable future?'

Career review or counselling (as discussed in the next chapter) will help those who desire promotion that cannot be offered or who have difficulty in career planning.

Systematic follow-up Unless agreed action regularly follows, an appraisal scheme is dead. Actions by the manager are likely to include training, support, changes to working practices, better communication, discussion with other managers or departmental heads and perhaps changes in personal style.

All these should be noted and their achievement monitored as closely as the achievement of the appraisee's targets.

The career development plan will naturally be reviewed and updated at each appraisal.

Action check-list
- Ensure that the aims and purpose of appraisal are necessary, achievable, consistent, agreed and understood.
- Promote the concept of an open, non-evaluative appraisal as an aid to career development and planning for all employees.
- Encourage full, visible commitment to appraisal from the top level.
- Devise simple paperwork and administrative procedures.
- Train both appraisers and appraisees fully, especially in effective interviewing.
- Develop and encourage the use of positive approaches for those not judged to have promotion potential.
- Monitor progress on agreed actions.
- Review the system regularly.

PERFORMANCE APPRAISAL

Why the scheme exists

The performance appraisal scheme is designed to:

- set medium- and long-term work objectives for each individual
- help monitor achievement against previous objectives
- identify and help solve any continuing work problems experienced by the individual
- help individuals to produce and review career development plans
- help establish development and training needs
- give managers feedback on their own performance
- help match the available skills, experience and interests to the overall needs of the organization.

The scheme does not in any way replace the normal, ongoing process of management, but provides a mechanism and an opportunity for individual and manager to devote time and effort to the review planning and development of the individual's career within the organization.

How the scheme works

All staff participate in the scheme. Each member of staff will be appraised by a nominated appraiser, who will usually be his or her direct manager or supervisor.

Appraisal is normally completed every 12 months, although there will be cases (such as following new appointment or where particular difficulties have been experienced) when it will be completed more frequently.

The process has the following elements:

1 completion of Form A by the appraisee
2 completion of Form B by the appraiser
3 exchange of copies of A and B between appraisee and appraiser a week before discussion
4 full discussion of the work of the *past* 12 months and plans and objectives for the *next* 12 months, based partly on the contents of Forms A and B
5 production (at the discussion or soon afterwards) of a list of work objectives for the appraisee and actions for the appraiser for the next 12 months
6 follow-up of all other agreed actions, including the implementation of training plans.

The administrative arrangements for the scheme are coordinated by
. . . . who will:

- establish the timetable in conjunction with management
- produce, issue, progress, collect and retain paperwork, maintaining confidentiality at every stage
- collate, record and draw to the attention of appropriate individuals problems and needs for action outside the responsibilities of individual appraisers.

Figure 10.1 An example of appraisal paperwork

Form A

To (the person being appraised). Please:

- think carefully about the questions and points below and any other aspects you feel are relevant to your work of the past 12 months
- write answers to each on the form
- pass a copy to (your appraiser) before (date one week before interview) and keep one for yourself
- read and think about the copy of Form B (appraiser) will let you have (Form B contains similar questions to those on this form)
- attend for a discussion with (appraiser) at (time) on (date) at (place).

What do you feel have been your achievements during the past 12 months?

_____

If objectives were set for this period [copies should be available] please say how far you believe you have achieved them.

_____

If you have experienced serious, continuing or unresolved problems during this period, please say what they were.

_____

What work objectives do you feel should be set for the next 12 months, considering the what, how and when for each?

_____

What personal development objectives would you like to set for the next 12 months? (Consider your long-term career direction, skills, qualifications, experience, responsibilities and any other factors that you feel are relevant.)

_____

What support do you feel you need from the organization in achieving both work and personal development objectives?

_____

Please mention any other aspects of the past or the coming 12 months that you feel are important.

_____

Figure 10.1   (continued)

Form B

To (appraiser). Please:

- think carefully about the questions and points below and any other aspects you feel are relevant to the work of (appraisee) during the past 12 months
- write answers to each on the form
- pass a copy to (appraisee) before (date one week before interview) and keep one for yourself
- read and think about the copy of Form A (appraisee) will let you have (Form A contains similar questions to those on this form)
- arrange for a discussion with (appraiser) at (time) on (date) at (place).

What do you feel have been (appraisee's) achievements during the past 12 months?

If objectives were set for this period [copies should be available] please say how far you believe (appraisee) has achieved them.

If there have been serious, continuing or unresolved problems during this period, please say what they were.

What work objectives do you feel should be set for the next 12 months, considering the what, how and when for each?

What personal development objectives do you feel would benefit (appraisee) in the next 12 months? (Consider (appraisee's) long-term career direction, skills, qualifications, experience, responsibilities and any other factors that you feel are relevant.)

What support do you feel you and the organization should give in achieving both these work and personal development objectives?

Please mention any other aspects of the past or the coming 12 months that you feel are important.

Figure 10.1   *(concluded)*

11 Mid-career evaluation: review and planning

Career development and planning activities have hitherto been largely a reaction to problems, whether for the employed or unemployed. It is now generally accepted that pro-active programmes are of great value to individual and organization. Such programmes may centre round one or more of a range of interrelated techniques, including performance appraisal, assessment centres, long courses, structured self-assessment, counselling and career development workshops. The aim of all of these is to facilitate the production and implementation of a development plan that can help move the individual from where they are now to where they wish to be in the future.

Individuals, managers, human resources professionals and outside specialists can all play a part in this process. Trainers may be directly involved in running career development workshops and possibly self-assessment programmes. If they are required to undertake counselling, they will need to be trained in the essential skills.

For the individual who is employed, career development and planning are the bringing together of the aspirations and skills of the individual and the needs of the organization. For those who are unemployed, the aim is to match their aspiration and skills with the employment opportunities available. For both groups the process has a key role.

Pro-active or reactive career planning?

Whether initiated by the individual or the organization, career review and planning have usually been undertaken as a reaction to redundancy or other form of job loss, unsatisfactory job performance, serious lack of job satisfaction or one of the other problems listed in Chapter 12. However, an increasing body of opinion sees pro-active career review and planning as a vital component in good human resources practice.

Strategic career development and planning programmes are based on the belief that career development planning is a major aid to the motivation and commitment of employees and (by guiding them towards jobs and functions in which they can maximize their job satisfaction and contribution) to the best use of the employer's human resources. Programmes may be targeted at groups of employees designated by age, function, level, sex or race or may be of general application.

Programmes will involve coordinated use of some or all of the techniques discussed below, probably in modules spread over a period of months.

The techniques of career review and planning

These may be diagnostic or developmental but most frequently combine elements of both. Some techniques are relevant only for those in employment, while others are of value both to them and to the unemployed. They include:

- regular performance appraisal
- assessment centres
- long courses
- structured self-assessment
- counselling
- career development workshops.

These activities can be undertaken pro-actively (as part of a strategic career planning programme) or reactively (in response to specific pressures or needs). They will contribute to the production of a career development plan (this is discussed in the second part of this chapter).

Regular performance appraisal

This has been discussed in Chapter 10.

Assessment centres

Assessment centres are physical locations at which a group is brought together, typically for two or three days, for a comprehensive programme of individual assessment. They may be used for the assessment of prior learning (APL) or prior experience (APE) in connection with the attainment of a qualification (see page 76), for recruitment (see page 34), for assessing promotion potential, or for career development and planning purposes.

The techniques used include psychometric tests, interviews and individual or group exercises. The programme will be designed to build up a systematic profile of each individual based on certain dimensions according to the purpose of the event and concept of personality used by those running the centre.

Assessment centres have come a long way from the techniques long used for selecting higher grade civil service and armed forces commissioned officer recruits. Several consultant organizations have specialized in their promotion in recent years and their use has grown rapidly. They are, however, expensive to run and, for this reason, generally considered practicable only for the senior employees of large organizations.

Long courses

Long management courses (see page 76) have for many years played a part in career planning in addition to the educational and training input. Some now include specific elements, such as the assessment and career counselling of participants. Most involve compiling reports on participants that can be used to assess promotion potential and development needs.

This method, derived from practice in the armed forces, is frequently linked to specific career stages. All employees who have reached a particular salary level or grade, who have been identified as having the potential to reach a particular level or who are listed for possible promotion to certain posts will be required to attend the appropriate course and undergo the related evaluation procedures. The method is very expensive and therefore invariably considered practicable only for more senior employees.

Self-assessment

Self-assessment is the most flexible basis for career development and planning. It is available to individuals whether in employment or not and may be incorporated as an element in other techniques, such as at an assessment centre or in career counselling.

The urge to develop and grow in adult life varies enormously between individuals and, indeed, within the same individual at different stages in their life. It is commonly assumed to diminish in strength from childhood to old age, but some people are more strongly motivated to continue developing past normal retiring age than others at the start of their career. For some teenagers, the urge is to earn and not learn; for some seventy- or eighty-year-olds the desire is to still grow to an ever fuller self-realization.

Whether or not an individual is subject to systematic appraisal, there is much value in occasional self-assessment. Commonly, such introspection may only occur in times of crisis, but it can be helpful as a starting point for new thinking or simply as a means of checking and consolidation at any time. An annual review, perhaps on a birthday or at the start of a new year, has much to recommend it.

A systematic approach to self-assessment provides a sound structure, generates creative thinking, limits unproductive emotional reactions and can offer benefits commensurate with those available from other assessment techniques.

There are a number of books and computer programmes available that can help (see page 125 for a simple but effective framework for self-assessment based on the concept of the Strengths, Weaknesses, Opportunities and Threats (SWOT) analysis).

Counselling

Career counselling is a major tool in career development. Most is now carried out following loss of employment, but counselling can be of great value throughout a career and is increasingly seen as an essential component in career development for all, whether in employment or not. In France, all employees now have the statutory right to independent career counselling.

Career counselling is a specialist activity requiring considerable skill and knowledge. There is danger in the belief that someone else can find a magic formula that will set us on the road to happiness and prosperity. No professional working in this field would make this claim, but many of those seeking help will have such a hope, even if it is only a subconscious one. Most experienced counsellors do not feel that it is their job to advise—rather, they work by helping their clients to learn about and face up to themselves, their personality, situation, strengths and limitations.

Counselling may be undertaken by line managers, human resources professionals or outside specialists.

The role of the manager

The individual's line manager is the natural first port of call for career counselling. Readiness to discuss problems—be they job or personal—is a requirement of good management. The manager will have the closest knowledge of the individual's working life and should have participated in appraising this regularly. The manager should also be well informed about the organization's needs and the opportunities it can offer. Whatever other arrangements may be made for career counselling, it would be disastrous not to benefit from the manager's input.

Whether counselling by the manager will be more effective than by a human resources specialist or an outside agency will depend on the difficulty of the problem, the nature of the management–subordinate relationship and the counselling skill of the manager. Counselling skills are heavily weighted towards effective listening and the adoption of a catalytic role—things that do not come naturally to every manager.

It is rare for managers to have the skills or time to devote to extended counselling. Employees may not, in any case, ask for such help—except in times of dire crisis or as a ploy to obtain some benefit. Some who feel the need for counselling may bypass their immediate manager because he or she is part of the difficulty or to maintain confidentiality. Alert managers will, however, be sensitive to the need for counselling and prepared to offer either their own services or those of some better-qualified member of the organization.

The human resources professional

Human resources professionals are frequently regarded by other employees as skilled and experienced counsellors as many readily accept the role and perform it well. However, counselling is skilled work in which the well-intentioned amateur is likely, at best, to be ineffective or, at worst, harmful. Trainers and other human resources professionals who are frequently called on to counsel should ensure that they are fully trained.

Outside specialists   A growing number of organizations and consultants offer help in career development. They cover:

- initial career choice
- ongoing career planning
- outplacement and job loss
- chronic unemployment.

Some professional organizations, such as the British Institute of Management, also provide these services for their members. A few telephone counselling and advisory services are available through subscription by employers.

These services may be paid for by individuals or employers. Some employers buy in a counselling service from outside providers as a benefit for their employees—particularly in cases of career difficulty or redundancy. However, the fees charged by external advisers may be very high and individuals who are unemployed and desperately seeking work should always be clear exactly what services will be provided. This is particularly important in the area of help in finding employment. It is illegal in the UK to charge individuals for finding jobs for them, but a few consultants may blur this fact and appear to offer services they cannot give.

Career development workshops

Career development workshops may be an ingredient in employers' career development programmes and are also provided by a number of independent consultants. They can be of value both to the employed and unemployed. They may be presented as a series or as self-standing modules, each of which are usually one or two days in length.

Typically workshops will cover such areas as:

- life and career planning
- self-assessment
- the job search
- c.v. preparation
- being interviewed.

The aims of career review and planning

Whatever methods are used, the ultimate aims of career development and planning are the same and may be summarized as answering three basic questions:

- 'Where am I now?'
- 'Where do I wish to be?'
- 'How can I get there?'

Where am I now?   The answer to this question is best found with the help of some framework for analysis, such as the SWOT analysis, which looks at strengths, weaknesses, opportunities and threats. A sample check-list for this type of approach is given in Figure 11.1.

THE PERSONAL INVENTORY

My strengths

What qualifications have I got?
What kinds of work have I done and for how long?
What special knowledge or experience have I got?
What skills do I possess? (A=high level, B=good, C=fair)
What resources of money or property do I have?
How wide is my fame and reputation?
Do I have strong support from my family or from friends?
Have I any other sources of power or influence?
How robust is my constitution and how good my health?
What are the strong points of my character and personality?
In so far as I have succeeded, what has helped me to do so?
Have I any strong, specific interests, either at work or outside?
What are the sources of my motivation and drive?
(Consider wealth, fame, security, independence, discovery, religious, political
or social conviction, family happiness, personal relationships, rivalry (with
whom?), fear (of what or whom?), etc.)
Under what circumstances have I felt happiest and most fulfilled?
Have I any specific unfulfilled ambitions; if so, what?
Have I strong emotional needs that I wish to satisfy; if so, which?
Have I other strengths not so far listed?

My weaknesses

Are there important gaps in my qualifications, experience or knowledge?
Have I financial difficulties?
Am I held in low esteem?
Have I enemies?
Do my domestic circumstances present any problems?
Have I health problems or physical disabilities?
What are the weak points of my character and personality?
Where I have failed, what has held me back?
Under what circumstances have I felt most frustrated and unhappy?
Have I other limitations not so far listed?

My opportunities

Am I aware of any specific opportunities for career development open to
me at the present time or that might be open in the foreseeable future?
(Consider organizational changes, retirements, departures or promotion of
others, business opportunities, job vacancies, the influence of friends willing
to help, successes I can capitalize on, prizes, scholarships, sponsorships,
bursaries, changes in the local or national economic climate or employment
situation, etc., and, wherever possible, give evidence.)

My threats

Am I aware of any specific threats to my present career situation, now or
in the foreseeable future?
(Consider organizational changes, possible redundancies or contraction of
the work-force, take-overs or mergers, closure or relocation of offices or
plants, the machinations of enemies wishing to harm, failures coming
home to roost, changes in the local or national economic climate or
employment situation, etc., and, wherever possible, give evidence.)

Figure 11.1   *SWOT-type sample check-list*

Where do I wish to be?

Completing the inventory honestly will, for most people, start the process of focusing and clarifying their thoughts and structuring an approach to the future. In so doing, many people find that:

- there are more and more valuable strengths in their position than they realized
- few weaknesses cannot be overcome or, at least, sidestepped
- the main battleground is the mind, will and motivation.

Without will and motivation, further development cannot take place. Those who are unemployed usually feel such motivation, at least initially, although the onset of discouragement and disillusion are the worst dangers of chronic unemployment.

Objective setting

Rational progress starts with the setting of aims and objectives towards which effort will be directed. Career development objectives cannot be confined to work as *all* spheres of life—including work, leisure and personal lives—are inextricably intertwined. Planning must, therefore, be for the whole person.

It is a common trap to start thinking about alternative courses of action before objectives have been defined. Objectives must come first and must be:

- clearly defined
- challenging
- attainable
- measurable.

Clear definition is vital. Committing the objective to paper usually helps to clear thinking and to eliminate ambiguity and vagueness.

Challenging objectives are motivating. They must have bite and offer the excitement of genuine achievement.

Attainable objectives must be set and they must be realistic. Impossible objectives will only serve to discourage.

Measurable objectives are important. Indeed, some people claim that unless an objective is measurable it is not worth setting. This *is* a counsel for perfection, but, none the less, the more clearly success can be defined the better.

An objective-setting check-list is given in Figure 11.2.

Alternatives

Having established objectives, it is possible to consider the alternative courses of action available and measure each against the objectives.

Alternatives can be classified under a number of headings:

- development within the present situation
- change (or obtain) job
- change of employer
- a sabbatical

OBJECTIVE-SETTING CHECK-LIST

These are thought starters only—you may well have nothing to enter in some boxes, but several answers in others.

Date drawn up	*Timescale for achievement:*		
	next month	*next year*	*lifetime*
Qualifications			
Achievements			
Family/relationships			
Status/position			
Money: income/ capital			
Property/ possessions			
Experiences			
Skills			

If a large number of objectives is produced, it may be necessary to prioritize them.

Figure 11.2 *A sample objective-setting check-list*

- change of career
- self-employment.

Development within the present situation will be a common outcome if the review process has not been undertaken under the pressure of a specific crisis. Thinking will turn at once to how the objectives can best be met (see page 129).

A job change may be indicated or, for the unemployed, the need to obtain a job.

For many who have exhausted what their present job can offer or found that it does not match their skills and needs, promotion will appear the most natural, perhaps the only avenue for job change. However, promotion is not an automatic solution, even when it is available. The trap of accepting promotion to an unsuitable job has ruined many careers. As mentioned previously, the 'Peter Principle' states all too clearly that many people are promoted until they reach their level of incompetence.

A sideways move—even occasionally downwards—may better meet the objectives. Accepting such an outcome will be a challenge both to the individual and counsellor (if there is one).

A change of employer may appear best. The grass will always appear greener on the other side of the fence, but before jumping over the wise person will want to be certain that it is not just a trick of the light.

Frustration with one's organization and boss are feelings shared, sadly, by a high proportion of employees. It is easy to misread feelings of this kind and be tempted into action that damages rather than furthers development. The most successful changes are more likely to be those taken for positive reasons ('I think that post is just right for me') rather than negative ('I must get out of here at any price').

The risks and opportunity cost of moving may, on occasions, outweigh any prospective benefits from a change.

The sabbatical is a period of time—frequently a year—during which employees are allowed, even encouraged, by their employers to take time off from their normal work and engage in something quite different; possibly an extended holiday.

It is currently only provided for senior members of academic institutions, but there is much to be said in favour of its more general use. It offers individuals the opportunity to rest, recharge their batteries, rethink their objectives and return to their labours once again bright-eyed and bushy-tailed. For the employer, such an approach could sometimes be right for an employee plateaued in mid career. It could prove more cost effective than either recruiting a replacement or allowing an otherwise highly satisfactory employee to become demotivated and progressively less productive.

Long training courses have typically been used as a sabbatical substitute for loyal, senior employees. While this may help the individual, their involvement can make the course less effective for other participants.

Career change was, until recently, considered the ultimate sign of failure—even now it may create suspicion, but the concept of a second career is increasingly accepted. The dangers of personal obsolescence and the frustrations of career plateauing after rapid early career development make this the best outcome for an increasing number of people.

Self-employment has been increasingly suggested as an appropriate form of career development in recent years, as the concept of the market economy has gained currency. It may have particular relevance in helping those whose career has plateaued to meet their objectives, possibly in the form of consultancy or other use of specialist skills and knowledge.

However, self-employment has dangers for those who have been in employment for many years and who have not developed the approach to risk taking, self-marketing and responsibility that it demands.

The development plan

From this analysis, a development plan can be produced. It will remain to consider how best the plan can be implemented and what help will be necessary to do this.

How do I get there?   The range of tools for mid-career development includes:

- the resources of their organization
- help from their manager
- training
- government schemes and initiatives
- continuing education
- the resources of professional and similar bodies.

Each of these has been discussed in the previous chapters.

If a change of job, employer or career has been decided, this will call for skills that may not previously have been developed. These will include:

- the techniques of job search
- c.v. preparation
- self-presentation and being interviewed.

The techniques of job   Job search, especially for the unemployed, calls for determination,
search   knowledge and a methodical approach.

Having decided to make the change, the personal inventory and list of objectives should help to clarify what kind of jobs are appropriate. It is then necessary to work methodically to:

- prepare a good c.v. and produce to a high standard
- scan local and national newspapers systematically for suitable vacancies
- scan trade and professional journals regularly
- register with the local Jobcentre Professional and Executive Register (PER)
- find and talk to any employment agencies or selection consultants who may be able to help (Yellow Pages is a starting point)
- target appropriate organizations and write unsolicited letters and enclosing the c.v.
- contact every friend and acquaintance who may be able to help and on whose discretion it is possible to rely
- contact trade or professional associations and check whether they can help in any way
- apply for all suitable vacancies.

It is essential *not* to:

- allow rebuffs and failures to discourage us
- pay a large sum of money to anyone to prepare our c.v.
- accept the help of consultants or advisers without knowing exactly what they will do and exactly what it will cost.

The claim made to job-seekers by a few career change consultants that 'the majority of senior jobs are not advertised' may be misleading; it is correct only because many such jobs are filled from within the organization and is not evidence that consultants hold a magic key to these vacancies.

C.v. preparation Possession of a sound, well-presented curriculum vitae is essential for all job-seekers. It may be of help to internal applicants in some organizations whose personnel records are not comprehensive or up to date. Help in c.v. preparation can be given by career development workshops and several books are available. Numerous individuals are ready to undertake preparation for a fee, but those who have access to a word-processor or a good typewriter and reasonable common sense should not need such help, for which grossly excessive fees are sometimes asked. An example layout is offered in Figure 11.3.

The c.v. should always be adapted in detail to individual job applications.

PERSONAL DETAILS

Name	John William Smith
Address	The Windmill, Spring Lane, Hightown HT3 6XC
Tel: (home)	0456 45251 **(work)** 0032 8787
Date of birth	20 February 1951 **Age** 40
Marital status	Married **Children** Peter (19)
	Jane (17)
Qualifications	BA (Hons) Modern Languages, upper second
	Fellow, Institute of Distribution Management
	Certificate of Professional Competence
	Member, Institute of Physical Distribution Management
Health	Excellent
Present job title	Distribution Manager
Present employer	XYZ International, plc
Present remuneration	£25,000+ car and benefits
Notice required	3 months

EDUCATION AND TRAINING

Schools attended
> 1955–1962, Hightown First School
> 1962–1969, Lowtown Comprehensive
> 1967,   O levels: eight subjects; 1969, A levels: French B, German B, History B

Full-time higher/further education
> 1969–1972, Sheffield University
> 1972,   BA (Hons) upper second, Modern Languages

Part-time/distance learning
> 1977–1978, Chartered Institute of Transport, Certificate of Professional Competence

Major occupational training
> 1973, Monsterco Systems Analysis practitioners' training
> 1985, Ashridge General Management Course

EMPLOYMENT HISTORY

Dates from/to	Name of employer	Job title
1987 to date	XYZ International plc	Distribution Manager

Responsible to Operations Director for all aspects of distribution. Six warehouses across southern England: fleet of 45 trucks, 30 cars; 150 personnel; annual budget £1.2m.

1981 to 1987	XYZ International plc	Warehouse Manager

Responsible to Distribution Manager for running of Southall Warehouse: 39 personnel; annual budget £250,000; final salary £18,500.

1978 to 1981	ABC Haulage Co Ltd	Fleet Manager (north)

Responsible to Managing Director for fleet of 12 trucks operating throughout northern England and Scotland on general haulage; final salary £11,250.

1973 to 1978	Monsterco plc	Systems Analyst

Responsible for customizing distribution software; final salary £8000.

1971 to 1973	Monsterco plc	Graduade Trainee

Final salary £5,500.

LEISURE INTERESTS

Cricket: playing member, Hightown Cricket Club.
Amateur dramatics: member, Bigborough Shakespeare Society.
Squash, tennis, marathon running (London Marathon, 1988).

Figure 11.3 *Example of a c.v. layout*

Plan implementation

Whatever the career development plan contains and whatever help is used, implementation will call for continuing strength of purpose by the individual if it is not to go the way of all New Year resolutions.

It is helpful to consider in advance what problems may afflict it and to decide whether we can

- prevent them
- prepare a contingency if they occur
- live with the result.

Commitment can be strengthened by revealing the plan to partners, close friends, managers or suitable colleagues.

It is essential to set review points for the elements in the plan, based either on elapsed time (monthly or possibly quarterly) or the attainment of key points.

Action
check-list
- Promote a pro-active approach to career development and planning.
- Coordinate all inputs to the career development and planning process.
- Encourage and train individuals to engage in structured self-assessment and career review at suitable intervals.
- Ensure that sources of effective career counselling are readily available for all who need them, especially in cases of job loss or other serious difficulty.
- If personally called on to counsel, obtain proper training.
- Provide career development workshops in needed subject areas.

12 Career problems—the individual

Careers may be blighted by problems specific to the individual or by problems that affect groups and classes. This chapter considers individual career problems, while Chapter 13 looks at those that can affect groups.

All afflicted by serious problems will benefit from counselling and the areas in which solutions are most commonly found and the chapters in which these are discussed are indicated at the end of each section.

Missing qualifications

Careers sometimes develop further, faster or in a direction that brings its owner up against the barrier of a missing qualification. This is most frequent in the early and middle stages—typically in the twenties and early thirties. It is easy to succumb to discouragement at this point, to the feeling that 'it is too late'.

The resources of open and distance learning and a number of special schemes are available to help those who have the will-power to use them. This is a situation in which the knowledge, support and encouragement of a skilled and informed trainer can be of enormous benefit. (See also Chapter 8.)

Under-performance

Chronic or serious under-performance will most naturally be dealt with initially by an individual's manager who may see it as a case for discipline. There are, however, circumstances that call for a more positive approach, including:

- an unexplained falling off by hitherto satisfactory performers
- specific problem areas for an otherwise good performer
- an unduly prolonged learning curve for a newly promoted employee.

In such situations the trainer and counsellor will often be able to help; correctable skill deficiencies may be discovered or personal, possibly health problems may be indicated. (See Chapters 5, 10 and 11.)

Boredom or staleness

Boredom and staleness afflict some, but by no means all, working in repetitive and routine jobs. It is a trap to project oneself into such a situation as some jobholders find it an ideal match for their own life-style. For others, however, lack of variety and challenge can be a killer.

If the latter situation is the case, the manager may be able to offer help in the form of job enrichment or job rotation. There may be the opportunity for a special assignment or secondment. Encouragement to undertake additional education or training may help, too. If the individual's ability and commitment are undoubted, early promotion may be the right answer. (See Chapters 5, 7, 8, 10 and 11.)

Under-used potential

This may produce the same symptoms as the previous problem, but is caused by the level of the work rather than its lack of variety. It is a classic problem afflicting anyone who has been over-sold on, or who has formed an unrealistic view of a job offer. Graduates seem particularly prone to the problem.

Those suffering may sometimes be diagnosed as lacking ability when, in fact, they have more than the job requires. Some may deliberately hide their feelings or even not realize their cause. Even trickier is the individual whose true potential has never been spotted or who is a late developer—what may be called the 'mute, inglorious Milton' syndrome.[1] Identifying and eliminating such waste of talent is one of the biggest challenges the career developer faces.

The initial identification of these problems usually lies with the manager, aided by the process of appraisal and review. (See Chapters 5, 10 and 11.) Progress depends on the selection and use of the most appropriate tools for mid-career development. (See Chapters 5, 6, 7, 8 and 9.)

Over-work

Chronic over-work can be a career killer. At senior level this can lead to 'executive burn-out', which manifests itself as severe deterioration in the performance of a hitherto achiever, possibly accompanied by ill health and other such indicators of stress. The problem can afflict careers at any level and the self-employed and those in smaller organizations often suffer badly.

It is generally supposed that young people are unlikely to experience this problem, or at least to be harmed by it, but this view may not be shared by young doctors.

Diagnosis and initial action usually lie with the manager but this problem often affects those who have no direct superior, in which case friends, colleagues and relatives have a responsibility. Professional counselling may be needed in serious cases. Simple over-work should be curable once diagnosed, but a sideways move, a sabbatical, a second career or early retirement may be options in chronic cases. (See Chapters 5, 11 and 14.)

Lack of prospects

The 'dead-end job' from which upwards escape is difficult or impossible, is an old chestnut at selection interviews, but a real and serious career problem for some. It is distinct from plateauing in that the limiting factor is the *job* rather than the *jobholder*.

Poor job and organization structure is often the cause, although bad selection may also be to blame. Managers sometimes turn a blind eye to the situation until it is drawn to their attention, perhaps during appraisal or review. (See Chapters 10 and 11.) If the individual is to be motivated and retained, promotion, if necessary by an unusual career path, will be called for. (See Chapter 9.)

Over-promotion

As there is a tendency for individuals to be promoted as long as they perform well and not promoted when their performance is unsatisfactory, most are likely to end their career in jobs in which they perform badly. There is devastating but not complete truth in this model.

When it occurs, over-promotion calls for strong, sometimes painful management action. However, the cause, in the shape of faulty selection, will almost always lie at management's door, so humility and humanity should be the order of the day. Sideways moves, special assignments, consultancy or early retirement will be among possible solutions. (See Chapters 5, 11 and 14.)

Boss problems

Managers who have not read or do not observe the principles and practices laid out in Chapter 5 are likely to have a devastating effect on the careers of those who work for them.

In this situation the individual is on a hiding to nothing and should seek the best and quickest way out. Skilled trainers will meanwhile do all they can to limit the damage by working on the boss. (See Chapters 5 and 7.)

Colleague problems

Just as the development of children is often more affected by their peers than by either teachers or parents, so are colleagues important in career development.

The dynamics of a working group are complex and influence every member of it. While some will be accorded the role of unofficial leaders, others may be seen as deviant or even become isolates—outcasts rejected by all. This group role will affect work performance and acceptability, not only to colleagues but to management. Group beliefs and attitudes about the organization and its management will also affect every member—indeed, many people have become chronically disillusioned and sought new jobs or employers solely because of the attitudes of close colleagues.

If sexism, sexual harassment, bad working practices or individual incompatibility exist within the group they, too, will form a major barrier to career development.

Help with such problems should be forthcoming from a wise and sensitive manager, aided as necessary by counselling and individual or team training in sensitivity or social skills. Improvement of job skills may help by eliminating causes of tension between colleagues (See Chapters 5, 10 and 11.)

Plateauing

The problems of plateauing are among the commonest in career development and have been increased by flatter organization structures, demographic trends, economic problems, mergers and reorganizations.

In fact, the simple arithmetic of the organization pyramid has always made the belief in the career as a steady climb to the top of a pyramid illusory: there have *never* been many posts in the next level up as there are people aspiring to fill them so it is physically impossible for more than a tiny proportion of even the most efficient and best-trained individuals to reach the top. Alistair Mant speaks graphically of the 'barrel' of middle-rank, middle-aged managers.[2]

Plateauing is sometimes spoken of in terms of the 'mid-life crisis' or, in sexist terms, as the 'male menopause'. The suggestion is that the whole personality and life-style of the individual is involved, rather than just the career. In fact, this is true of all stages of the career, with the tensions of early family life and impending retirement being far worse than those of the mid-career stage for many people.

However, the tensions of plateauing can be particularly damaging for certain personalities. From seeing their career as progressive, successful and purposeful, they are faced, often quite suddenly, with a feeling of utter failure. From this can develop self-doubt, a serious falling off in performance, symptoms of stress, health problems and chronic depression. Plateauing may cause a feeling of shame, even guilt. There may be a refusal to accept its reality and its effects can quickly extend to personal and family life. Many are unable to find an appropriate and positive response.

Plateauing must, of course, happen to all. The variables are the age at which it strikes and the reaction of the individual. Unskilled workers may plateau at any age from the teens onwards. Those with well-developed skills and good qualifications will usually plateau later, while technical and professional people may plateau as early as the late twenties. Managers usually plateau between their early thirties and late forties. It is often assumed that the more talented will plateau later, but this is by no means always true. For example, some fast track managers have burnt out—even risen to the top—by their mid thirties. Equally, as with the unplanned child, unexpected promotion may occur to anyone at almost any age.

Facing the plateau is most difficult for those who have seen their career in what we have called the military model—the climb to the top of a pyramid. Looking always upwards, they will have failed to see the comfortable ledges and cosy niches on which the majority have found their happiness. They will not have realized how few are actually standing, like archangels on the point of a needle, at the top, nor how cold the wind up there can blow. Plateauing, therefore, is only a problem for those whose career model is at fault.

In practice, individual and organization frequently satisfy each other's promotional urges by a sort of ritualistic dance involving annual salary rises, juggling with job titles, organizational status symbols, responsibilities and occasional more major reorganizations. That the feeling of forward and upward movement is often illusory can be verified by those who have the courage to check their career-long salary at constant money value.

Those who have special difficulties in coming to terms with plateauing need help, not only for their own good, but for that of the organization as they form a potent source of bad morale. This help must begin with sensitive diagnosis by the manager. The organization can offer help through job rotation and changes in job structure designed to maximize the contribution the individual can make and—most importantly—*feel* they are making. In some cases, skilled counselling will be needed, often aimed to draw together the threads of working, personal and leisure lives and to widen the individual's range of thinking. For some, reconciliation to the positive possibilities of planned early retirement or a second career will prove the answer. (See Chapters 5, 6, 11 and 14.)

Wrong choice of career

The realization that years of time and effort have been invested in a less-than-optimum career can be shattering. Many fight against the conclusion, finding it too hard to face, but the chance to put things right exists for far longer, up to a far greater age, than most realize—especially today when second careers have become fairly generally acceptable.

Counselling can be of great help, especially when followed by guidance on the substantive help available from education and in other ways. (See Chapters 8 and 11.)

Wrong choice of organization

Individual styles and cultures may clash with organizational styles and cultures—especially at senior level, where it is possible for transplants to fail completely. Thorough, two-way recruitment methods are the best prevention. Cure can be difficult and the danger of career harm is very real. (See Chapters 3 and 11.)

Family and personal problems

Marital breakdown, bereavement, third-party illness or accident and the many other shocks this flesh is heir to can have devastating effects on work performance and on long-term career prospects. The need to care for ageing parents or disabled relatives, to provide the best educational and social background for one's children, to match one's own career moves with those of one's spouse or to balance career against social and leisure interests affect many. The match (or mismatch) between personal and domestic responsibilities and the needs of career development can be one of the most severe tensions felt by an individual, frequently leading to failure, or felt failure, in either or both spheres. Such tensions may be either the effect of or cause of alcohol or drug abuse.

Such problems often come to a head in such ways as deciding whether to take on additional commitments of time or responsibility and whether to move home. The cycles of family and career development often run parallel in time with, for example, children being born at just the moment when the first major career development opportunities occur.

While career development must always be closely linked to personal development, the relationship is not simple and depends on the nature of the career and the demands of the life-style. A brilliant artist, for example, may have failed to develop even adequate life skills; a top manager may have failed to develop as a satisfactory parent or spouse.

It is, of course, true that family life can also bring immense career benefits. The support it can give is the bedrock of many of the most successful careers. To translate an old proverb into non-sexist form, we can perhaps say that 'Behind every successful person is a good partner'.

When there are problems, sensitive diagnosis by the manager is essential, followed by counselling and whatever tangible help—revised hours, reduced responsibilities, compassionate leave and other options may be available. Drug or alcohol abuse, especially in an employed adult, are now generally seen as conditions requiring treatment. (See Chapters 5 and 11.)

Clashes between organizational and individual interests

This conflict is illustrated by 'indispensable' employees who are denied development opportunities by their employers because they are too valuable where they are. In the crudest form, such treatment is probably rare, but in the sense that employers and managers may choose to retard rather than accelerate individual development, it is probably common.

As with some other aspects of career development, such problems are often at their most severe for those working for smaller employers who may be unable to offer opportunities for promotion and may lack the resources to develop and train.

Trainers will do whatever is open to them to press the case for development and individuals will be alert to the possibilities of self-improvement. (See Chapters 6, 7, 9 and 11.)

Job loss

The principal causes of job loss—dismissal, resignation, redundancy and organizational bankruptcy affect careers in different ways, but the danger of subsequent unemployment is the same for all. Some individuals claim that 'redundancy is the best thing that ever happened' to their career, in the sense that it jerked them into action from a rut of complacent inactivity. For many more, however, it is a grave problem and the seriousness of the situation increases with age—over the age of 40 it may prove to be the ultimate disaster.

The individual's chances, at whatever age, are greatly enhanced by practical and moral support. Responsible employers will offer outplacement support. For the individual, counselling is available from private agencies, although this may be expensive and of variable value. In the later stages of employed life, understanding of the satisfactions of the various approaches to retirement may be the best approach. Government-sponsored help is available in several ways. (See Chapters 8, 11 and 14.)

References

1. *Elegy in a country churchyard*, Thomas Gray.
2. Mant, Alistair, *The Experienced Manager—a Major Resource* (BIM, 1969).

13 Career problems: collective difficulties

There are a number of common problems that can afflict careers which are beyond the control of their owners. These include sexual discrimination, racial discrimination, discrimination by age, other forms of discrimination, industrial relations issues, location and organizational history.

While some of these have deep-seated social causes, trainers can use their influence against the attitudes that cause these problems, especially when training managers.

Discrimination is one of the worst career blights. It is type-casting, judging people by the group they belong to rather than as individuals. It shapes careers in many ways, especially by its effect on recruitment, opportunities for development and promotion. It can occur in many different forms, of which sexual and racial discrimination have been the subject of legislation.

Sexual discrimination

In the opinion of many people, sexual discrimination is the most serious bar to the development of meaningful careers that exists, affecting as it does over half the work-force.

Discrimination based on sexual stereotypes can affect careers in many ways: recruitment, rates of pay, opportunities for development and training, returning after childbirth, dual-career couples and retirement.

While sexual discrimination is most often suffered by women, men who wish to progress in traditionally female-dominated areas, such as secretarial and the caring occupations, may also experience it, as a growing number of Industrial Tribunal cases shows.

Sexual stereotypes

Social conditioning from the earliest age inhibits many men and women from even attempting to develop careers outside the conventional sexual roles.

Stereotyped thinking suggests that men are, on average, stronger, taller, more intelligent, more aggressive, less caring and less tolerant than women. The perceived difference in some dimensions, such as average strength, is clearly justified, but the perceptions of others, such as average intelligence, are not. Whatever the averages, however, discrimination occurs if someone is judged as a member of a class rather than as an individual. Probably the most damaging stereotypes are the pervasive myths reinforced daily by the media of the weak, temperamental woman and the strong, assertive man.

Job stereotyping suggests that air hostessing, typing or nursing are 'women's work' while bus driving, welding, legal or engineering are 'men's work'. Such thinking effectively bars many careers to one sex or the other.

Stereotypical thinking is not restricted to employers, but is reinforced by individuals and society as a whole. Many women, for example, are extremely reluctant to consider traditionally male jobs and the reactions of family, friends and neighbours often reinforce such doubts.

Recruitment The Equal Opportunities Commission has, with the authority of law, striven to eliminate discriminatory practices but most observers feel that much remains to be done.

Many male managers and employers remain obsessed with the belief that all young women are likely to 'leave to have children'. While this can be true, it is of far less significance than some still insist on assuming. Many young women now delay having children and some choose to have none. Of those who do, an increasing proportion decide to return to work at the earliest moment, sometimes only weeks after the birth. The chances of a young woman leaving a post to have a child are probably little if any greater than those of a man leaving for any of a range of other reasons.

Rates of pay Despite several attempts at legislation (such as the Equal Pay Act 1984) the impression remains that there is widespread wage discrimination against women.

Development and training There are substantial discrepancies in the development training opportunities offered to the sexes. The Equal Opportunities Commission reports[1] that among younger workers, men are one and a half times more likely to receive job-related training than women. In another recent study,[2] the Equal Opportunities Commission found that more than three fifths of YT places were occupied by boys, that only 1 in 5 16–18-year-old girls received job-related training as against 1 in 3 boys and that less than a third of the 16–18-year-olds given day- or block-release by their employers were girls.

Promotion The problems here mirror those in initial recruitment. In most occupations, women have more difficulty in obtaining promotion than men and the more senior the post, the greater the difficulty. Studies have shown that while women form 45 per cent of the UK work-force, they account for only 11 per cent of general managers and less than 1 per cent of chief executives.[3] Those who do progress find increasing difficulty in what becomes a more male-dominated environment with every step up.

Women returners   The biological imperatives of childbearing inevitably make the development of female careers harder attitudinally as well as physically.

The legal right of mothers to return to their job within a designated
time after childbirth is established in the UK, but whether a continuing
career can or should be combined with bringing up children remains a
battlefield. Some (many of whom are women) believe it is practically
impossible and morally wrong to attempt the combination. Others
believe that, as soon as possible after the birth, the rearing of children
should become just one factor in the woman's career pattern and not
necessarily the predominant one.

Women seeking to pick up their career after a period of full-time
domestic duties face a formidable array of difficulties. Against them are
ranged sexism, ageism, personal and technical obsolescence, lost confidence, child-care problems, the expense of retraining or education, the
general discrimination against all not following a standard career path
and the difficulties afflicting all who have been out of paid employment
for a long period.

For those with toddlers, the provision of crêches by employers and
other child-minding services are essential. The problems of a family of
school age remain—in the view of many parents—intractable unless
domestic help such as a grandparent or reliable *au pair* is available. Even
children at boarding schools must return during holidays. The phrase
'latch-key kids' has been coined to describe those who must return, after
school, to an empty house and who are generally felt to be at risk from
such an arrangement. The suggestion that, to minimize this problem,
schools should remain open (staffed by auxiliary helpers) until about 6
p.m. has recently been revived. Part-time or flexible working hours and
job-sharing arrangements can help but may not take account of school
holidays.

Home-working got a bad name from the start of the Industrial Revolution
due to the merciless exploitation of those who did it, but conditions are
different now. The ever-increasing resources of information technology—micro computers and telephone data links—can help house-
bound parents in many occupations. The pioneering work of Steve
Shirley in setting up her network of home-based computer programmers—F International—has formed a model for many others.

Updating for women returners will, in many cases, call for further education and providers will need to ensure that age and other entry
requirements are so framed as not to preclude them. Polytechnics and
the Open University offer Associate Student status, which allows students to study single units from a course. BTEC provides continuing
education qualifications and there are no age limits for them. The CATS
scheme has been mentioned in Chapter 8 (see page 96). Colleges of
further and higher education offer Access courses, aimed at helping
adults to move quickly onto the qualification ladder.

Specially targeted personal skills training, notably in assertiveness and other aspects of self-presentation, are offered by many providers to women wishing to return.

Dual-career couples

If both partners wish to continue their career, they may experience both difficulties and advantages.

The difficulties of maintaining a sound personal relationship prove substantial for many couples, especially if the career requires extensive travelling or periods away from home. They also face problems when the opportunities for one clash with the needs of the other, especially if relocation is involved. Traditionally the male career has taken precedence, but for an increasing number of couples this is no longer automatic.

The second income helps solve child-rearing problems by, for example, enabling the employment of domestic help or sending children to boarding school. This flexibility can also extend to the choice of which partner is to continue their career at any given point and which will accept the bigger share of the household duties. However, social attitudes to the househusband are still developing and for many the leap is too great.

Retirement

The most serious form of discrimination against men is the differential state retirement age of 60 for women and 65 for men. By requiring five extra years from the male working life, this gives men an average of 11 or 12 fewer years of retirement than women.

The converse form of discrimination also occurs if a woman is forced to retire at an age at which men are allowed to continue working, although this has now been made illegal within the UK.

Racial discrimination

The effects of racial discrimination on the career prospects of ethnic minorities are too well-known to need elaboration here. As with sexual discrimination, legislation has been in place for a number of years and the situation is monitored by the Equal Opportunities Commission.

In the view of many, the problems remain as formidable as ever and progress in most areas is discouragingly slow. Numerous studies have confirmed that the unemployment rate for black people in the UK remains about twice that for whites. An unpublished study carried out for the Department of Employment[4] indicates that, although nearly twice the proportion of Asians aged between 16 and 18 complete education and training than this age group of white young people, they have only half as much chance of getting a job as whites of the same age with equivalent qualifications. Mary Coussey and John Whitmore have shown[5] that many aspects of recruitment methods, including word-of-mouth recruitment, inconsistent standards, unnecessary job requirements and undue reliance on internal promotion within a predominantly white work-force, have built-in bias.

Career development and planning

Section 37 of the Race Relations Act 1976 allows training to be mounted specially for members of a particular racial group where this group has been under-represented in a particular field of work. The Pepperell Unit of the Industrial Society works in all areas of gender, race and disability, seeking to develop individual potential and organizational effectiveness. It mounts courses, workshops and conferences for employers, undertakes advisory and consultancy work, runs conferences for schoolchildren and students and workshops for career advisers.

Age discrimination

The arbitrary discrimination between individuals by virtue of their ages is blatant and unjustifiable but very common. Typically, person profiles for vacancies and the resulting advertisements include statements such as 'below the age of 40', 'mid thirties' and so on. Even when such limitations are not declared, candidates of certain age groups will be automatically ruled out by selectors. Usually, an upper limit is specified, with 35 or 40 being common and occasionally a lower limit being set. Studies of job advertisements indicate that the optimum age for nearly any job application lies between 30 and 35, with the number of openings falling steeply above the age of 40 and virtually disappearing when 50 is reached.

Like other forms of discrimination, age discrimination is based upon crude stereotypes. It is claimed that mental flexibility becomes lower with age, making adaptation to new or changing conditions harder. It is suggested that older employees are unlikely to work well with a 'young team'. Older people are claimed to be outdated in their knowledge and skills. Those who have failed to reach particular career benchmarks by a certain age are supposed to have shown their lack of ability. Older employees cause strains on the arrangements for pensions and life insurance.

As with all kinds of discrimination, older people deserve to be considered not as members of a class but as individuals. Ageing affects individuals at different speeds and in different ways, so some people are 'older' at 30 than others at 80. A glance at leaders of world class—from General Woolf (17) and Pitt the Younger (25) to Churchill and De Gaulle (80+)—is instructive in this respect.

Age discrimination imposes much tighter limits on career development than is often realized. Because job opportunities peak in the early thirties, it is by this age that most progress must have been made. Most individuals will then be between 10 and 20 years into their career and will normally have between 20 and 30 years left. The proportion of the career that has elapsed before further progress becomes difficult will thus vary between a maximum of half and a minimum of as little as a quarter.

The straightjacket thus imposed is one of the biggest obstacles to rational career development. Those who naturally develop more slowly or who are starved of opportunities in the early stages are likely to find themselves trapped. Faced with the urgent need to escape, they may be forced into an error of judgement, choosing a job or an employer that blocks further progress. Those who make it to the top *before* their mid thirties, however, are not exempt from career development problems: 20 years with nowhere else worth going to is more than most enjoy, even if they *are* the boss.

That people as young as 30 may be subject to ageism has been revealed in a study by the University of Strathclyde[6] that Barbara Graham presented to the Institute of Personnel Managers. She also found that mature graduates were less likely to be considered for vacancies, especially in manufacturing, finance and the media, although the civil service, local government and education authorities and charities showed less such discrimination.

On the other hand, as reported at the same conference by Peter Monaghan,[7] the Operations Director, B & Q stores found that employees over 50 years of age are '. . . more patient, more friendly, more enthusiastic and more knowledgeable' than many younger staff and the company planned to increase the proportion of such employees substantially.

Age discrimination is (within broad limits) illegal in the USA and a number of other countries are considering similar legislation.

Older employees may suffer discrimination in other ways than recruitment and promotion. Unable to afford jeopardizing their pension position and with no chance of getting another job, they may be denied training opportunities and put into jobs or otherwise treated in ways that younger people would not accept.

Other forms of discrimination

Discrimination can occur in almost any situation. The phrase 'blue-eyed boy' implies discrimination in the form of favouritism. Discrimination by visual characteristics, such as clothing and hair style, is also common.

Discrimination by experience

Experience in an area of work is commonly called for in internal or external job advertisements. In the computer function, for example, several years' experience may be required of particular applications of particular software on particular machines.

Such requirements may appear justified, but can also make life difficult both for organization and individual. The field of applicants will be severely limited, making the job harder to fill and restricting the career development opportunities it offers. Training of an otherwise suitable individual may often produce better long-term results than insistence on arbitrary experience.

Undue emphasis on experience results in individuals becoming type-cast early on in their careers, to the disadvantage of them and their organizations. Some organizations (as, for example, parts of the Civil Service and some nationalized or once-nationalized industries) and

some functions (notably selling) less frequently impose such requirements.

The old school tie

The effects on career development of membership of clubs, societies
and other organizations is often mentioned. These may be variations of
the 'old school tie' syndrome or suggest the supposed effect of more
hidden relationships. The Masonic Orders are frequently hinted at,
usually with little evidence.

There can be no doubt that such influences do affect careers, but their
effects are probably greater in some than in others. There is little individuals can do but understand their working and act as their conscience
dictates and political skills allow.

Discrimination against disability

Those suffering certain disabilities suffer grave and unjustified discrimination that frequently has a disastrous effect on their career development. These include spastics, those who are partially or totally blind or
suffer from epilepsy, the effects of certain illnesses and physical injury
or deformity. AIDS sufferers, in particular, currently experience
immense prejudice. The attempts by the various charities working on
behalf of these groups to educate employers about the real effects and
the real potential of such people have so far done little to lessen the
immense barrier of prejudice and misunderstanding they suffer.

Industrial relations issues

Trade unions have done much to affect the career development both of
their members and of others working in related areas. By granting or
withholding membership, they have often controlled those who were
able to follow a given occupation.

It is sometimes said that 'you can't get an acting job without an Equity
card, but you can't get a card without an acting job'. The need to limit
entry to a grossly overcrowded occupation and to preserve the
opportunities of those already within it is generally accepted to justify
such restrictions, but the possibility of abuse is also clear.

While closed shops have been rendered illegal within the UK, the concept continues, in practice, to exercise influence due to the attraction to
some employers of the tidiness of the arrangement.

The conflict between active support of a trade union and the career
offered by one's employer has proved hard for some, especially among
active union members in middle management and the human resource
function.

Unions have, in some cases, sought to exercise control over promotion.
The changes in industrial relations climate and legislation within the UK
in recent years has probably made such cases rarer, although some
managers may still feel an indirect pressure on their decision making.

Location and geography

In the world of county cricket, it is said that a Middlesex player has a better chance of being picked for England than someone playing for, say, Somerset. Geographical location inevitably has a strong influence on career development, with London still being the centre of commercial activity, despite moves to encourage businesses to set up in other areas of the country.

The mobility of labour

The continuing increase in personal mobility has brought about major changes in choice of occupation. In general it has made choices easier and more flexible at every stage. Fewer people live over the shop and, over the last century, commuting distances have lengthened from a mile or two to over a hundred. Cross-country travel away from the major centres and the traditional routes has become easier. The growth of second homes has enlarged the areas of job choice for individuals and families.

Despite these factors, mobility of labour remains patchy and practical difficulties face individuals, organizations and government with almost intractable problems. Improved transport facilities have sometimes accelerated the drain of employment from a region, rather than stopping it. The high cost in the south-east of Britain makes moving into it extremely difficult. Council housing policies, together with the low volume of private rented accommodation, add to the obstacles.

A study by Tony Fielding[8] concludes that many people in recent years have deliberately started their career in the south-east of England where promotion to well-paid posts is most readily obtainable and moved, often in their early forties, to areas of cheaper housing such as mid Wales, the south-west and rural Yorkshire. In doing so, they have often abandoned their first, successful career and used the capital they accumulated to become self-employed or to buy a small business.

The industrial history of particular areas devoted to mining, cloth manufacture, vehicle manufacture and so on still has some effect. However, it has been much reduced by such factors as the replacement of heavy industry (cotton and woollen cloth, steel, shipbuilding and so on) by imports, the exhaustion of raw materials, or their replacement, by imports (coal, iron ore and so on) and the development of sophisticated and more efficient physical distribution systems and direct government action designed to diversify industry, aid depressed areas and relocate large Civil Service offices.

The European Community

The enlargement of the European Community has already had an influence. Its final completion in 1992 will have a fundamental effect on careers at every level. Liberalizing the flow of labour throughout the Community will act directly, enabling all to sell their skills in a huge market. Conversely, the competition for work in some occupations and areas will become fiercer. Employment and social legislation is already undergoing a process of harmonization that will have a major impact on education and training, qualifications, conditions of employment (especially for disadvantaged groups), recruitment and retirement practice. (See also page 96).

Organizational geography

In any widely-dispersed organization, some locations are likely to be less popular than others due to their remoteness and the travel difficulties they cause, the nature of the work done, the unpleasantness of the environment, the state of the buildings or the character of some of the people who work there. Fortunate, indeed, those who work in a location that people like to work in and visit—be it London, Brussels or Barbados.

To work in an organization's headquarters makes people unpopular, but can help their careers. A plethora of higher-graded jobs will offer more career opportunities. Those at HQ will be better known to top management and thus more likely to receive developmental attention than those labouring out in the Styx. Many large organizations deliberately bring high-flyers into HQ for a period in order to enhance their development.

On the other hand, balanced career development suggests periods away from HQ and the more popular locations. The need for wide experience of the work, people and environment of an organization calls for periods at a variety of locations. Such movement will often allow chances to manage small operations at an early career stage.

History

Organizational history can do much to harm career development. Most large organizations have developed through a series of mergers and take-overs and the personal and political tensions of such events are often far-reaching and long-lasting and extend far outside the boardroom. The opportunities for career development of those working within the junior partner of a take-over may be damaged—possibly permanently—by the desire of the senior partner to impose its style, ethics and methods of working.

'That's not the way we do things here . . . .' Industries acquire attitudes towards job design that can become almost impossible to break. The content and nature of most long-established jobs are usually defined by tradition so that continuity becomes security, not only for the jobholders, but for their managers. It is instructive to compare the content of jobs such as those of the railway engine driver and commercial airline pilot and the extent to which tradition has determined the sources of recruitment, method of training and career development of each. A methodical study would probably throw up some remarkable conclusions.

Action check-list

- Make managers aware of the harm done by sexual, racial, age and other forms of discrimination.
- Help and encourage those women employees who wish it to plan for a resumption of their career after childbirth.
- Train recruiters in sound, discrimination-free procedures.
- Become familiar with and draw others' attention to effects on career development of the completion of the EC in 1992.
- Ensure that trainees gain experience both of HQ and operational units.
- Work to minimize the harm done by cultural differences between the partners in any merger involving your organization.

References

1. 'Training for women—the future imperative'. Equal Opportunities Commission Report, 1990.
2. Reported in the *Financial Times*, 30 November, 1990.
3. 'Guardian Royal Exchange survey', quoted by Lorna Bourke in the *Independent*, 17 November, 1990.
4. Unpublished Department of Employment report, quoted by Nick Tester in the *Independent*, 28 October, 1990.
5. Coussey, Mary, and John Whitmore, *Jobs and Racial Equality* (British Institute of Management, 1987).
6. 'Removing the age barrier—the mature graduate', paper by Barbara Graham, presented to the Institute of Personnel Management, reported in the *Independent*, 26 October, 1990.
7. 'Removing the age barrier—Case Study 2 B & Q', paper by Peter Monaghan presented to the Institute of Personnel Management, reported in *The Daily Mail*, 26 October, 1990.
8. Paper by Tony Fielding presented at the Institute of British Geographers Annual Conference 1991 and reported in the *Independent*, 4 January, 1991.

14 Retirement

Retirement on the grounds of age has traditionally been seen as the conclusion of the career. However, an increasingly flexible view is taken of the situation so that now many continue to develop their careers long after such an event—often producing new and deeper working satisfactions. The decision as to whether retirement is to be an end, a beginning or just another stage is clearly a part of career development.

Training professionals are actively involved in preparation for retirement and pre-retirement training. They are also a natural source of advice, counselling and support.

More parties are involved in retirement than in any other aspect of career development. They include:

- the individual
- the family
- the manager
- the training professional
- the organization
- voluntary agencies
- pensions and other financial institutions
- local government
- national government.

The importance of pension arrangements can detract from the attention paid to the other, sometimes even more critical psychological and developmental aspects of the change. Some organizations may even feel that scarce resources should not be devoted to this aspect of career development. Besides its obvious importance to the individual, however, a positive and supportive view of retirement is of immense value in maintaining commitment and motivation in the later years of employment.

Policy should be based on the most flexible approach possible, taking account of the range of options open and the needs of each case.

What is retirement?

Retirement may be compulsory in that individuals may (or may not) wish to go on working, but the employer does not allow them to do so because they have reached an agreed retirement age.

Most employers now provide an age band during which retirement may take place. This may be from the age of 65 down to 60, 55, or even as low as 50. During this period, the employee is usually able to decide to leave without losing pension benefits. Some employers may retire employees compulsorily during this period, effectively as a form of redundancy.

Women have gained the right to remain in employment until the age of 65. Some employers are prepared to offer continued employment to men or women after normal retiring age, subject to the continued need for their skills. A flexible approach to the age of retirement is becoming commoner, to the benefit of employer and employee.

The provisions of private pension schemes vary widely and may be flexible. State pensions are based on the fixed retirement ages of 65 for men and 60 for women, a rigid and discriminatory arrangement causing many problems for individuals. The full state pension is also only payable to individuals who have made a statutory minimum amount of contributions during their employed career. Private pensions will be unaffected by any subsequent employment or earnings, but the state scheme has complex rules covering the various possible situations.

Length of retirement

When the state retirement pension was first established in the UK, in 1908, the retirement age for a man was, as now, 65. The expectation of life for a male, at birth, was a little over 66 years. The legislation was thus based on the likelihood of death following retirement, on average, within about one year.

While the state retirement age has been held at 65 for men and 60 for women, the life expectation for men has risen to about 78 and to 82 for women. Thus, on average, men may now look forward to about 13, and women about 22 years of retirement. It is now possible for retirement to exceed the length of time in employment.

The advantages and disadvantages of retirement

As with promotion, retirement is not automatically advantageous—either to employer or individual.

The advantages for the employer

Retirement opens posts for new jobholders. Indeed, if the retiree holds a senior post, the chain reaction may affect all levels below. If the retiree's work has become sub-standard, retirement offers the chance to find a better replacement.

The drawbacks for the employer

Retirement may deprive the employer of an experienced employee who possesses rare and expensive skills—the distillation, in fact, of career-long development. Such experience and skills may prove difficult to replace.

The advantages for the individual

To the individual, retirement offers freedom from the routine, effort and responsibility of work. It offers flexible use of time for leisure or whatever purpose the individual may choose. It offers the chance to move home to a place of their choice. It may be beneficial to health.

The drawbacks for the individual

The drawbacks include a sudden drop in income and loss of the companionship, sense of purpose and status given by a job. It may place substantial strains on the relationship with the partner (being continuously in each other's company often proves an unhappy experience even for the most stable couple). The psychological effects—particularly the loss of sense of purpose—can be serious; retirement, it is said, is the biggest killer of all.

From the angle of the state, retirement turns a net contribution to the economy by the worker into a net drain by the retiree.

There should, thus, ideally be nothing automatic about retirement: flexibility has everything to recommend it to both parties. Effective development will depend, as at previous career stages, on sound evaluation of the situation and the best use of all the available options. The one thing that can be said is that complete, arbitrary and compulsory retirement is likely to do more harm than good.

After retirement: the working options

The increasing length of retirement has led many individuals to see a long and satisfying retirement as a key aim of their employed life. In the past, retirement meant total withdrawal from paid employment, but today this is increasingly only one of a range of options.

Paid employment

Some retirees grasp the opportunity to take other employment, sometimes effectively starting a further career. Those who have retired in their fifties may choose to obtain new, full-time employment, perhaps at a lower organizational level—a retired manager, for example, driving a minibus. Alternatively they may fill a role that uses their accumulated skills and experience, possibly with a rival organization or one whose work is complementary to that of their previous employer. A few make a completely new departure, using different skills, knowledge and interests from their previous career.

Modern information technology is an increasing help. The use of micro and modem can enable individuals to engage in the work of an organization they may hardly ever visit—a cottage in the Yorkshire Dales may be as sensible a work-station as the next office.

Some retirees opt for part-time work, perhaps as a local collector, cashier or salesperson. Their previous employer may wish to use them, possibly in their previous area of work, either on a regular basis or to cover sickness, holiday and other absences.

The self-employed   Many retirees choose to set up their own businesses. Frequently this may be some form of hospitality, say, a café, boarding house, bed and breakfast establishment or pub.

Those with craft skills may exploit them—perhaps for the first time—to their own direct advantage. Some turn to writing or other media work; a few buy a smallholding.

Internal consultancy   Some organizations are able to offer posts to employees at retirement as consultants or advisers on a fee-paying or retainer basis. This can help employers and also enable employees to put their experience and skills to best effect while being relieved of the routine and responsibility that they no longer relish. Such arrangements are more common in larger organizations and for more senior employees. There may be scope to extend them to a wider range of levels and job types.

External consultancy   Many of those who retire from more senior posts, at whatever age, call themselves 'consultants' after they have done so. This covers a range of situations—from the nationally known figure whose days are filled with highly remunerative assignments for organizations of all kinds to those who are simply not yet able to come to terms with their new situation.

Many areas of expertise including, sadly, most aspects of human resource management, are densely crowded with those wishing and able to give advice. Unless the individual has a national reputation or at least one captive client to start with—typically their ex-employer—the chances of a heavy work-load are limited. In less well-provided-for areas, consultancy will have a greater likelihood of success, but marketing will always need at least as much effort as the work itself.

Voluntary work   Many retirees engage in some form of charitable, organizational, political or other voluntary work. They may use their career skills by, for example, keeping the books of a club or acting as its secretary. Some will find fulfilment in totally new fields, perhaps by entering local politics or becoming actively engaged in fund-raising or some form of voluntary social work.

Study   The development of open learning has vastly widened the study options for people in later life. Apart from the satisfaction of researching some pet area of knowledge, it is now practicable to obtain additional (or initial) qualifications at any age through the Open University and other distance learning methods.

Preparation for retirement

Preparation for retirement during the later years of employment has been generally accepted as the responsibility of the employer. It has been undertaken largely as a social duty, but also as a means of maintaining the commitment of employees during the last years of their employment. Whatever the age retirement takes place and whatever the final job of the retiree, provision of such assistance is a final act of career development by the grateful and responsible employer for the loyal employee.

Pre-retirement training has been offered by an increasing number of employers. Some life assurance companies and other financial advisers have also seen advantage in involvement in such work. Training has more frequently been offered by larger organizations, but is now available through public courses to all.

The armed forces probably offer the clearest and most thoroughly developed example of pre-retirement training and the one with the longest history. Members of the forces can, in effect, retire at almost any age, depending on their rank and the terms of their contract, but the majority leave during their forties, with many years of economically active life ahead. The same is true of professional sports men and women and others whose first career depends on a high degree of physical strength and skill.

Pre-retirement training should be started well in advance of the likely age of retirement—preferably at least five years. A modular basis, in which the first module is aimed to focus the attention of individuals positively on what is often an unwelcome prospect, has much to recommend it. This can be helped by drawing attention at this time to the range of working options.

The first module will also provide a natural opportunity to offer individual counselling. This sometimes proves a sensitive area and will need a particularly delicate touch. It is ideal if one counsellor can retain contact with the retiree throughout the period. While financial counselling may be helpful, control of this work should not be in the hands of purely pension or financial advisers.

The later training modules will cover areas such as:

- relationships with spouse, children and friends
- leisure activities and life-style generally
- educational opportunities
- private and state pension arrangements
- money management and investments
- social security benefits
- physical and mental health
- place of abode.

Action check-list

- Take a pro-active role in organizational retirement policy making and practice.
- Ensure that the importance for the organization as well as for the individual of positive and supportive retirement policies is widely understood.

- Guide all concerned towards a flexible approach based on the circumstances of individual cases.
- Counsel individuals towards successful retirement throughout the later years of employment.
- Ensure that good pre-retirement training is given, starting several years before the likely date of retirement.

Useful organizations

British Association for Commercial and Industrial Education (BACIE)
16 Park Crescent, London W1 4AP Tel: 071-636 5351
British Institute of Management (BIM)
Management House, Cottingham Road, Corby NN17 1TT Tel: 0536 204222
Business and Technician Education Council (BTEC)
Central House, Upper Woburn Place, London WC1H 0HH Tel: 071-388 3288
The Careers and Occupational Information Centre (COIC)
Moorfoot, Sheffield S1 4PQ Tel: 0742 704563
The Careers Research and Advisory Centre (CRAC)
Bateman Street, Cambridge CB2 1LZ Tel: 0223 354551
Centre Européen Développement Formation Profession (CEDEFOP)
Bundesalle 22, D-1000, Berlin 15, Germany Tel: 030 88 41 20
City and Guilds of London
76 Portland Place, London W1 4AA Tel: 071-278 2468
Council for National Academic Awards (CNAA)
344/354 Gray's Inn Road, London WC1X 8BP Tel: 071-278 4411
Department of Education and Science (DES)
Elizabeth House, York Road, London SE1 7PH Tel: 071-934 9000
Department of Employment
Caxton House, Tothill Street, London SW1H 9NF Tel: 071-273 3000
Educational Counselling and Credit Transfer Information Service (ECCTIS)
PO Box 88, Walton Hall, Milton Keynes MK7 6DB Tel: 0908 368924
Engineering Council
10 Maltravers Street, London WC2R 3ER Tel: 071-240 7891
The Equal Opportunities Commission (EOC)
Overseas House, Quay Street, Manchester M3 3HN Tel: 061-833 9244
The Foundation for Management Education (FME)
Sun Alliance House, New Inn Hall Street, Oxford OX1 2QE Tel: 0865 251486
The Human Resource Development Partnership (HRDP)
16 Park Crescent, London W1 4AP Tel: 071-636 5351
The Industrial Society
Peter Runge House, 3 Carlton House Terrace, London SW1Y 5DG
Tel: 071-839 4300
Industry Matters
8 John Adam Street, London WC2N 6EZ Tel: 071-930 9129
Institute of Personnel Management (IPM)
IPM House, Camp Road, London SW19 4UX Tel: 081-946 9100
Institute of Training and Development (ITD)
Marlow House, Institute Road, Marlow SL7 1BN Tel: 0628 890123
Institution of Industrial Managers (IIM)
Rochester House, 66 Little Ealing Lane, London W5 4XX Tel: 081-579 9411

Management Charter Initiative (MCI)
(See NFMED, below).
National Council for Vocational Qualifications (NCVQ)
222 Euston Road, London NW1 2BZ Tel: 071-387 9898
National Economic Development Office (NEDO)
Millbank Tower, Millbank, London SW1P 4QX Tel: 071-217 4000
National Forum for Management Education and Development (NFMED) and The Management Charter Initiative (MCI)
Little Adelphi, 10 John Adam Street, London WC2R 0DW Tel: 071-257 3412
National Examination Board in Supervisory Management (NEBSM)
76 Portland Place, London W1 4AA Tel: 071-580 3050
National Institute of Adult Continuing Education (NIACE)
19B De Montfort Street, Leicester LE1 7GE Tel: 0533 551451
National Institute of Careers Education and Counselling
Bayfordbury House, Lower Hatfield Road, Hertford SG13 8LD Tel: 0992 558451
Occupational Research Centre (ORC)
The Hatfield Polytechnic, Birklands Annexe, London Road, St Albans AL1 1ED
Tel: 02072 79781
Pickup Programme
Room 2/2, Department of Education and Science, Elizabeth House, York Road, London SE1 7PH Tel: 071-934 0888
Pre-Retirement Association
19 Undine Street, Tooting, London SW17 8PP Tel: 071-767 3225
Production Engineering Research Association (PERA)
Nottingham Road, Melton Mowbray LE13 0PB Tel: 0664 501501
Project Trident
The Trident Trust, 91 Brick Lane, London E1 6QN Tel: 071-375 0245
Replan
19B De Montfort Street, Leicester LE1 7GE Tel: 0533 551451
Royal Society for the Encouragement of Arts, Manufacturers and Commerce (RSA)
8 John Adam Street, London WC2N 6EZ Tel: 071-930 5115
School Curriculum Industry Partnership (SCIP)
Centre for Education and Industry, University of Warwick, Westwood, Coventry CV4 7AL Tel: 0203 523951
School/Industry Forum
DES, Elizabeth House, York Road, London SE1 7PH Tel: 071-934 9314
Scottish Vocational Education Council (SCOTVEC)
Hanover House, 24 Douglas Street, Glasgow G2 7NG Tel: 041-248 7900
Teaching Company Directorate
Sudbury House, London Road, Faringdon SN7 8AA Tel: 0367 22822
Technical and Vocational Education Initiative (TVEI)
236 Grays Inn Road, London WC1X 8HL Tel: 071-278 0363
Training Access Points (TAPS)
Tap Unit, TEED, St Mary's House, c/o Moorfoot, Sheffield S1 4PQ
Tel: 0742 527344
Training Enterprise and Education Directorate (TEED)
Moorfoot, Sheffield S1 4PQ Tel: 0742 594178
Workers Educational Association (WEA)
Temple House, 9 Upper Berkeley Street, London W1H 8BY Tel: 071-402 5608
Young Enterprise
Ewart Place, Summertown, Oxford OX2 7BZ Tel: 0865-311180

Career-development initiatives

Initiative	Contact
Training/education funding, loans	LEAs, TECs, Department of Employment
Education/training opportunities, information	TAPs, Career offices
Vocational qualifications/ training	NCVQ/NROVA, TVE I
Employment training	Department of Employment, TECs
Small business training	TECs
Open/distance learning	Open University, Open College
Professional development	Appropriate professional body
General information	BACIE, BIM, BTECH/SCOTVECH, COIC, CRAC, Department of Employment, PICKUP, TEED

Bibliography

Ball, Ben, *Manage Your Own Career* (British Psychological Society with Kogan Page, 1989).

de Board, Robert, *Counselling People at Work* (Gower, 1983).

Fletcher, Clive, and Richard Williams, *Performance Appraisal and Career Development* (Hutchinson, 1985).

Gleeson, Denis, *Training and Its Alternatives* (Open University Press, 1990).

Hall, D.T., *Careers in Organizations* (Goodyear Publishing Co., Pacific Palisades, California, 1976).

Harrison, Robert F., and Richard M. Vosburgh, *Career Development for Engineers and Scientists* (Van Nostrand Reinhold, New York, 1987).

Harrison, Rosemary, *Training and Development* (Institute of Personnel Management, 1988).

Healy, Charles C., *Career Development* (Allyn and Bacon Inc., Boston, 1982).

Herriot, Peter, *Recruitment in the 90s* (Institute of Personnel Management, 1989).

Kaufman, H. G., *Obsolescence and Professional Career Development* (AMACOM, 1974).

Leighton, Patricia, and Michael Syrett, *New Work Patterns* (Pitman, 1989).

McGoldrick, Anne, and Gary L. Cooper, *Early Retirement* (Gower, 1988).

Peel, Malcolm, *Management Development and Training* (PPL, 1984).

Peel, Malcolm, *Readymade Interview Questions* (Kogan Page, 1990).

Rogers, Bill, *Careers Education and Guidance* (CRAC Hobsons, 1984).

Sidney, Elizabeth, and Nichola Phillips, *One-to-one Management* (Pitman, 1991).

Super, Donald, and J. A. Bowlsbey, *Guided Career Exploration* (Psychological Corporation, New York, 1979).

Super, Donald E., *The Psychology of Careers* (Harper & Row, 1957).

Watts, A. G. (ed.), Donald E. Super, and Jennifer M. Kidd, *Career Development in Britain* (CRAC Hobsons, 1981).

Wood, Sue (ed.), *Continuous Development, the Path to Improved Performance* (Institute of Personnel Management, 1988).

Woodruffe, Charles, *Assessment Centres* (Institute of Personnel Management, 1990).

Directories and handbooks

Alston, Anna, and Ruth Miller, *Equal Opportunities—a careers guide* (Penguin, 1987).

Baird, Robert B., *The Corporate Directory of Career Change and Outplacement* (Executive Grapevine Ltd, 1990).

Bayley, Julie, *How To Get a Job After 45* (Daily Telegraph and Kogan Page, 1990).

Brown, Rosemary, *Good Retirement Guide* (Gerald Duckworth & Co. Ltd, 1988).

The Careers Adviser's Handbook (Newpoint Publishing Co. Ltd, annual).

DOG (Directory of Opportunities for Graduates) (Newpoint Publishing Co. Ltd, annual).

GET (Graduate Employment and Training) 1991 (CRAC Hobsons, 1991).

GO (Graduate Opportunities) (Newpoint Publishing Co. Ltd, annual).

Handbook of Careers Information in the UK (Careers Consultants Ltd, 1987).

The Job Book (CRAC Hobsons, annual).

Kemp, John, and Bill Tadd, *The Macmillan Handbook for Retirement* (Macmillan, 1987).

Korning, Margaret, *Training for Your Next Career* (Blue Arrow PLC and Rosters Ltd, 1989).

Pates, Andrew, and Martin Good, *Second Chances* (Careers and Occupational Information Centre, 1987).

Returning to Work (Women Returners' Network and Kogan Page, 1990).

Segal, Audrey, *Careers Encyclopedia* (Cassell, 1987).

The Training Directory 1991 (Kogan Page in association with Bacie, annual).

Yearbook of Adult Continuing Education (National Institute of Adult Continuing Education).

Index